EVERY WAR   HAS TWO LOSERS

At the Bomb Testing Site *Portland, Dec 1953*
~~Testing the Bomb~~
At the ~~Testing~~ Site

~~Near Las Vegas~~
~~(or Dutchman's Flat)~~
~~Frenchman's Flat~~

At noon in the desert ~~with~~ a panting lizard

wai~~ting~~ *d* for history, its elbows tense,

watching the curve of a particular road

as if something might happen.

It was looking at ~~it was near~~ *something* farther off
~~those people could see, an important scene~~
~~picturing~~ it as an important scene,
~~acted in stone for~~ ~~~~ *little pelvis*
~~more for the world as less for myself,~~

at the flute end of consequences.
Here
was
~~I was~~ just a continent without much on it

under a sky that never cared less.

~~Ability~~ ready for a change, the elbows ~~promised~~ *waited.*
~~at the rocks origin/herds~~ *the desert*
~~something more than just waiting.~~

#
New Yorker, Partisan, Poetry,
NMexQ, Sewanee, Harpers, Pac.
Spect., Perspectives USA, Colo
Quarterly, W~~estern Review in~~
~~Dec 155~~
~~Atlantic~~ *Liberation would*
like later
accepted by Talisman
in Feb 1957

Typescript with manuscript alterations, "At the Bomb Testing Site," published in William Stafford's first poetry collection, *West of Your City*, in 1960.

EVERY WAR
HAS TWO
LOSERS

———◆———

WILLIAM STAFFORD
ON PEACE AND WAR

Edited and with an
Introduction by
KIM STAFFORD

milkweed
editions

Published 2003 by Milkweed Editions
Printed in the United States of America
Cover and interior design by Christian Fünfhausen
The text of this book is set in Garamond.
10 11 12 13 14   8 7 6 5 4
First Edition

"Atwater Kent," in *How to Hold Your Arms When It Rains* (Lewiston, Idaho: Confluence Press,
1990). Copyright © 1990 by William Stafford. "Men," "Poetry," and "Pretend You Live in a
Room," in *Even in Quiet Places* (Lewiston, Idaho: Confluence Press, 1996). Copyright © 1996
by The Estate of William Stafford. Reprinted with permission from Confluence Press.

"For the Oregon House Session" in *Crossing Unmarked Snow* (Ann Arbor: University of
Michigan Press, 1998). Copyright © 1987 by William Stafford. "You and Art" in *You Must
Revise Your Life* (Ann Arbor: University of Michigan Press, 1986). Copyright © 1986 by William
Stafford. Reprinted with permission from the University of Michigan Press.

Selected poems from *The Way It Is* (St. Paul, Minn.: Graywolf Press, 1998). (For a complete list
of poem titles, please see the acknowledgments on page 167.) Copyright © 1960, 1962, 1966,
1970, 1975, 1976, 1977, 1982, 1983, 1984, 1987, 1991, 1998 by William Stafford and the Estate of
William Stafford. Reprinted with permission from Graywolf Press.

All other material is published with permission from the Estate of William Stafford.

Milkweed Editions, a nonprofit publisher, gratefully acknowledges support from the Bush
Foundation; Henry and Emilie Buchwald; John Cowles III and Page Knudsen Cowles;
Dougherty Family Foundation; Joe B. Foster Family Foundation; Furthermore, a program
of the J. M. Kaplan Fund; General Mills Foundation; Jerome Foundation; Dorothy Kaplan
Light; Marshall Field's Project Imagine with support from the Target Foundation; McKnight
Foundation; Minnesota State Arts Board through an appropriation by the Minnesota State
Legislature; National Endowment for the Arts; Navarre Corporation; Debbie Reynolds; St. Paul
Companies, Inc.; Ellen and Sheldon Sturgis; Surdna Foundation; Target Foundation; Gertrude
Sexton Thompson Charitable Trust; James R. Thorpe Foundation; Toro Foundation; United
Arts Fund of COMPAS; and Xcel Energy Foundation.

Library of Congress Cataloging-in-Publication Data

Stafford, William, 1914–1993
　　Every war has two losers : William Stafford on peace and war / edited and with an introduction by Kim Stafford.—1st ed.
　　　　p.　cm.
　　Includes bibliographical references.
　　ISBN 1-57131-273-0 (alk. paper)
　　　1. Peace—Literary collections. 2. War—Literary collections. I. Title: Every war has 2 losers.
　　II. Stafford, Kim Robert. III. Title.
　　PS3537.T143A6 2003
　　303.6'6—dc21
　　　　　　　　　　　　　　　　　　　　　　　　　　　　　　　　　　　　2003000530

This book is printed on acid-free paper.

FOR THE PEACEMAKERS
OF MY FATHER'S GENERATION
AND OF THE GENERATIONS TO COME.

MAY THIS BOOK BEFRIEND
YOUR LIFE OF WITNESS.

EVERY WAR HAS TWO LOSERS

Editor's Note

In editing this unusual book, I have chosen in many instances to represent my father's unpublished writing exactly as he penned it in the early morning, alone with his thoughts. The language is sometimes very compact, the thought line intuitive, and the effect both intimate and challenging. The poems are represented as he revised and published them, and most of the interviews he had a chance to review. Some of the Daily Writings, however, were never revised, and they live here with you in their native form. I invite you to read these as they were written: attentive, deliberate, in a spirit of welcome as thoughts come forth.

EVERY WAR HAS TWO LOSERS

THESE MORNINGS

Watch our smoke curdle up out of the chimney
    into the canyon channel of air.
The wind shakes it free over the trees
    and hurries it into nothing.

Today there is more smoke in the world
    than ever before.
There are more cities going into the sky,
    helplessly, than ever before.

The cities today are going away into the sky,
    and what is left is going into the earth.

That is what happens when a city is bombed:
    Part of that city goes away into the sky,
    And part of that city goes into the earth.
And that is what happens to people when
a city is bombed:
    Part of them goes away into the sky,
    And part of them goes into the earth.

And what is left, for us, between the sky and the earth
    is a scar.

Los Prietos
20 January 1944

What Is Left for Us

An Introduction by Kim Stafford

Is it naive to seek for national and international security through poetry? My father believed it is naive to seek with weapons of steel. Behind the strife of nations, there is another way. This way is individual, collective, and universal. This way feels the wounds of any war, but looks beyond.

> And what is left, for us, between the sky and the earth
>   is a scar.
>   —*from* "These Mornings"

When my father, the poet William Stafford, wrote "These Mornings" it was January of 1944. He had just turned thirty, and he was living in a camp for conscientious objectors in the mountains of California. He and his pacifist companions were fighting forest fires instead of killing and being killed by the young men of Germany, Italy, or Japan. This was before the big Allied bombing campaigns—Berlin, Dresden, Tokyo, and finally Hiroshima and Nagasaki—but already my father saw the scar that would be left for us. His poem is eerily relevant to what was left at Ground Zero in New York City in September 2001—the scar in the ground left by the death of thousands on the wrong side of someone's anger, and the scar in our national psyche with all its military consequences of reprisal. It is relevant also to the scars left among the people of distant lands where our own bombs have fallen.

What would it be like for a thoughtful member of the Taliban to write a poem of compassion for the victims of the attack on the World Trade Center and the Pentagon? What would it be like for American poets to write of their compassion for the families of the fanatics—or the families under the rain of bombs intended for the Taliban or Saddam Hussein? In his published and unpublished writings my father showed it is possible—and crucial—to think independently when fanatics act, and to speak for reconciliation when nations take sides.

All his life William Stafford was witness for a comprehensive view. He believed in the fragile but essential community of the world, and he wrote on behalf of what he called "the unknown good in our enemies." In his view, such a life of witness was both compassionate and profoundly practical—in the long term, wars simply don't work as well as reconciliation. So every day of his life, from those years in World War II until his death in 1993, William Stafford would rise before first light to remember, to ponder, and to write—often writing about peace and reconciliation.

It would be difficult to overestimate the unusual importance of William Stafford's daily writing practice. Most of us read or hear the daily news, beginning each day with a dose of another person's truth. My father had a different way: to *create* the news of our common life by writing your own. This act is true freedom and constructive citizenship. It is available to all of us.

From Stafford's morning writings, and from poems,

statements, and interviews that grew from his thinking about reconciliation as it developed in those mornings, I with others have assembled this book ten years after his death. My father's pacifist writings speak to us directly—including both published poems and many passages from his daily writings not previously published.

Every country needs generous conversation among differing views. This book provides an alternative approach to a nation's military habit, our government's aggressive instincts, and our legacy of armed ventures in Europe, the Pacific, Korea, Vietnam, the Persian Gulf, Afghanistan, and beyond.

What is the place of writing, and a life of witness, in national affairs? Our nation has a founding document, the Declaration of Independence. In our first war, we defended the sentiments of that document with a military revolution. We killed for those self-evident words. Some of those who did not join the killing were called traitors, and were shunned. Thus, our beginning.

My family, by contrast, has a founding story. Sometime around 1920, the young William Stafford came home from school and told his mother that two new students had been surrounded on the playground and taunted by the others because they were black.

"And what did you do, Billy?" said his mother.

"I went and stood by them," Billy said.

No one knows how my father got to be that way. His brother became a bomber pilot in World War II. His sister married a navy man. But as a child my father somehow arrived at the idea that one does not need to fight; nor does one need to run away. Both those actions are failures of imagination. Instead of fighting or running you can stand by the oppressed, the frightened, or even "the enemy." You can witness for connection, even when many around you react with fury, or with fear.

In this belief, Stafford wrote each day, and often his writing included specific considerations of human connection. His daily writing included instructive dreams:

> I am in an army and we are in a place like a stadium and are supposed to start fighting; but we look at each other and somehow just don't quite get started. Then we realize that maybe we won't have the war. I am aware of the chancy nature of things—if we can keep from frightening each other, maybe it all won't start.

He had personal experience with the chancy nature of human interaction. Such experience made him thoughtful, and in his early morning writing he often began with a single sentence, one he never made part of a poem or otherwise published. We call these his aphorisms:

> Every war has two losers.

> The wars we haven't had saved many lives.

> You may win a war you are sorry to have started.

When I come upon these lines in the archive of my father's work, I wonder why he never gathered them himself. (He called his unpublished work his compost pile.) Sometimes these isolated statements show a quirky humor:

> Children of heroes have glory for breakfast.

> The Militarist's Farewell: Good-bye, Boomerang, see you later.

Children playing with knives.
Children swearing. Children
running a country.

For the most part, his writing is not accusatory, but inclusive. He knows he is caught in our great human charade, and he struggles to step outside and see things in an independent way:

Fool that I am, I keep thinking things will work
out, that we can coast along while injustice prevails,
and somehow it will change.

It began to dawn on me how weak and fallible
people are, how habits and limited environments
had fostered institutionalized smugness and vainglory: when saber-toothed tigers died out bravery
began to be possible; lack of association with superior sensibilities allows the assumption that we apprehend all that is around us; success at customary
activities enables us to assume that we are in control
of anything we put our minds to. This mirror that
we admire will shatter if touched by any of the real
rocks around us.

As he continues writing every morning, his words might begin to gather momentum as a poem:

If you don't know the kind of person I am
and I don't know the kind of person you are
a pattern that others made may prevail in the world
and following the wrong god home we may miss our star.

—*from* "A Ritual to Read to Each Other"

If my father achieved his most lasting and public utterance in his poems, I believe the cradle of those poems was his habit of living apart from narrow patriotism in a way made possible by his pacifism. This book shows what it is like to live in a mind where pacifism prevails, where mother country is the world.

Every War Has Two Losers is a collection of considerations that step outside the confines of nationality, politics, narrow patriotism, and other ways of life that imprison the imagination. If you live outside, on your own, you do not see the people of the world as loyal citizens or as enemies. You see them as individuals, as parents, neighbors, and friends—or potential friends. You begin to ask absolute questions:

> Save the world by torturing one innocent child?
> Which innocent child?

Standing outside the frenzy of your country's ways, you inquire about the complexities behind the news of winning, as in this statement Stafford published in the summer of 1991, at the conclusion of the Gulf War:

> Is there a quiet way, a helpful way, to question what has been won in a war that the victors are still cheering? Can questions be asked without slighting that need to celebrate the relief of a war quickly ended?
> Or does the winning itself close out questions about it? Might failing to question it make it easier to try a war again?
> Maybe a successful performance that kills tens of thousands, that results in the greatest pollution in history, that devastates a nation, that helps confirm governments in the reliance on weapons for security—maybe such an action deserves a cautious

assessment? Maybe some people might be forgiven a
few thoughtful moments amid the cheering?

Much of my father's oblique view of American history,
policy, and militarism was formed in the unusual company
of the CO camps during World War II. In selections from
interviews gathered here, Stafford talks about his friends in
the camps who taught him new ways to consider the military
decisions being made quickly in the wake of Pearl Harbor:

> There was a fellow named Hidarro Herrera from
> Coyote, New Mexico, and he could speak a little
> English, and I asked him about his draft board.
> He said they asked him, "Why are you refusing
> to go to war?" And he said, "God don't like war."
> So, where do you go from there? What could you
> ask next?

Included in this book is a chapter from my father's account
of life in those camps, his 1947 book *Down in My Heart,*
with its report of his near hanging at the hands of American
patriots. But even about such an adventure, my father is
thoughtful, and a student of human process:

> It takes such an intricate succession of misfor-
> tunes and blunders to get mobbed by your own
> countrymen—and such a close balancing of good
> fortune to survive—that I consider myself a rarity,
> in this respect, in being able to tell the story, from
> the subject's point of view; but just how we began
> to be mobbed and just where the blunders and mis-
> fortunes began, it is hard to say.

Toward the end of his life my father wrote of the quiet
heroes of his world—the champions not of war but of

reconciliation—in words that I take to describe his own presence:

> In the center of human life are those who hold it together. They make home what it is. They listen to "leaders," receive, decide. Whatever country is, whatever a profession, a town—they establish that.

With much help, I have shaped this book to sustain people who hold life together. As a father, as a teacher, as a citizen of the world, I intend to do what I can to raise up a generation in the spirit of peace. All around us, it's war, terror, reprisal. But we may step aside, invited to join each other on the path of peace by my father's words before dawn.

The Mob Scene at McNeil

———

A Chapter from *Down in My Heart*

The Mob Scene at McNeil

" W hen the mob comes," George would say, "I think we
should try surprising them with a friendly reaction—
take coffee and cookies out and meet them."

"As for me," Larry would say, "I'll take a stout piece of stove
wood, and stand behind the door, and deal out many a lumpy
head—that's what they'd need."

"Well, I don't know about you all," Dick would say, "but
I intend to run right out of that back door and hide in the
brush—'cause I don't want my death on any man's conscience."

When are men dangerous? We sat in the sun near the depot
one Sunday afternoon in McNeil, Arkansas, and talked cor-
dially with some of the men who were loafing around in
the Sabbath calm. Bob was painting a watercolor picture;
George was scribbling a poem in his tablet; I was reading
off and on in *Leaves of Grass* and enjoying the scene.

When are men dangerous? It was March 22, 1942. The
fruit trees at the camp farm were in bloom. We had looked
at them as we went by, starting on our hike, and we stopped
while I took a picture of George and Bob with our two little
calves. We spoke of the war and of camp and of Sunday
as we hiked through the pine woods and past the sagging

houses. We knew our way around; we had done soil con-
servation work during our months in camp, in the fields
beside our path. Not all had been friendly, it is true. Our
project superintendent had warned us against saying "Mr."
and "Mrs." to Negroes, and we had continued to use the
terms; and one stormy night when no doctors would come
out, some of the men in camp had given first aid to a Negro
woman, whose husband had led them through the dark
woods to the cabin where the woman lay screaming. Thus
we had become friends with some of our neighbors. With
some of them we had made friends, but it was harder with
others, and we went to town inconspicuously, with care, no
more than two at a time; and we were in most ways the quiet
of the land, and unobserved, we thought.

When we had hiked into McNeil we had found a few
men loafing around in the shade. The stores were closed;
Main Street extended a block each way from the depot and
then relaxed into a sand road that wandered among scattered
houses. We too relaxed for our Sunday afternoon. Bob set up
his drawing board; George got out his tablet and pen; and
I sat leaning against a telephone pole and began to read—
among dangerous men.

It takes such an intricate succession of misfortunes and
blunders to get mobbed by your own countrymen—and
such a close balancing of good fortune to survive—that
I consider myself a rarity, in this respect, in being able to
tell the story, from the subject's point of view; but just how
we began to be mobbed and just where the blunders and
misfortunes began, it is hard to say. We might have lived
through a quiet Sabbath if it had not been for Bob's being
an artist; or, especially, if it had not been for George's poem;

and on the other hand we might have become digits in Arkansas's lynching record if Walt Whitman had used more rhyme in his poetry.

About eight of the townsmen gathered to look over Bob's shoulder as he painted. His subject was a dilapidated store across the street. The men were cordial and curious. I asked them questions about their town. The only time we were abrupt was when they asked where we were from. "Magnolia," Bob said, and quickly changed the subject to their town baseball team. One of the onlookers edged up behind George and looked over his shoulder, while George went on with his composing and revising—unheeding.

I went back to my book, and I'll never be able to remember whether I was reading, when it happened, "Come, I will make the continent indissoluble. . . ."

I looked up. The onlooker, a handsome young man, well-dressed, and with tight skin over the bridge of his nose, had snatched George's poem and was reading it.

"What's the idea of writing things like this?" he challenged. "If you don't like the town, you haven't any right to come around here." I was familiar with the edge on his voice. He knew we were COs.

George stood up, straight, with his arms hanging at this sides, his face composed, and remonstrated that he hadn't meant the poem to be read—he was just trying to write, trying to express his own feelings.

"Here," George said, "I don't want the poem; I'll take it and throw it away." The young man held the poem away from George's outstretched hand and took his discovery a few steps away to show it to another townsman. The two muttered. The first man returned. He scrutinized Bob's drawing, while George and I stood without moving and Bob went on painting—a little faster. What could we do when men were dangerous?

The young man spoke, not directly to us but to the other townsmen, some of whom had drawn nearer, about our being COs. There was more muttering, in which we began to hear the quickening words—"yellow" and "damn." At first these words the men said, about us, to each other; then the faces were turned more our way when the words were said. A short, strong man broke into action, went to where Bob was still sitting, and grabbed the drawing board.

"Why, sir!" Bob said, and looked up as if in surprise.

"We'll take care of this," the short man said. He started to rip the drawing paper from the board, but another man stopped him.

"Save that for evidence." The short man raised the board over his head to break it over a piece of iron rail set like a picket near the depot; then he stopped, considered, caressed the board, and settled down to hold it under his arm and to guard the evidence.

"We ought to break that board over their heads," someone suggested. Several others repeated the idea; others revised the wording, expanded the concept, and passed the saying along. Some spoke of "stringing them up."

George got constructive. "I guess I'll go home," he said; "I don't think they like me here." He started to leave the circle—by now there were about fifteen men around.

"Hey, you; you're not going any place," one said.

"Don't let him leave," said another.

George came back and sat down.

A man at the edge of the group—a beautiful man to

us—said, "Let's call the sheriff." This call was in turn echoed around. To our great relief someone actually crossed the street to call. The tension, however, was far from ended.

The young man who had started the inquisition turned to me. "What were you doing?"

"I was reading a book." I held it up—*Leaves of Grass.* "A poetry book."

"What's that in your pocket?" he asked, pointing to my shirt pocket. I explained that it was a letter which I had written.

"But you said you hadn't written a letter," he accused. The group of men shifted their feet. I explained that I had been reading a book immediately before, but that earlier I had written a letter. The questioner demanded it, arm out-stretched. The others were watching these exchanges, some-times retiring to the edge of the group to talk and then elbowing back. By now about twenty-five were present.

The questioner considered and then accepted my sugges-tion that he wait for authority before taking the letter. He turned away, and he and others tried to argue with George about his convictions on war. George wouldn't say much—just that he considered war the wrong way of attaining ends many agreed to be good.

Then the young man veered, in the midst of the discus-sion of war, to an accusation that George's writing was not poetry. There was an implication that if it wasn't poetry it might be something else—like information for the enemy. George said that he thought what he had written—it was being circulated constantly through the crowd, exciting rumbles of anger wherever it passed—was poetry, and that poetry didn't need to rhyme. This opinion brought snorts from the crowd. The young man said that poetry always rhymed. *Leaves of Grass* throbbed under my arm, but I said nothing.

Drawing down one side of his mouth and looking sideways at George, the young man said, "Where did you go to school?" He grabbed the book from under my arm and opened it at random. He read a passage aloud to the lowering group, to prove that poetry rhymed. He started off confidently, read more and more slowly, and finally closed the book with a snap.

"Well, that may be poetry," he said, "but what you wrote ain't." The crowd was a little taken aback. It shifted its feet.

By this time I had a chance to look over a shoulder and read George's poem, which I hadn't yet seen. It certainly was unfortunate—a Sandburgian description of McNeil beginning, "McNeil! Humph! Some town, McNeil. . . ." An alert bystander clucked at a line in the poem: "And loaded freighters grumble through at night."

"There!" he said. "That's *information.* That's them troop trains!" We lost all we had gained from Whitman.

By this time, though, some of the group were arguing about why Bob painted. None of them could understand his insistence that he painted for fun. "But what are you painting *that* for?" they asked, pointing to the old store building. "It must be for a foreign power," one said.

"I don't think a foreign power could use a picture of this store in McNeil," Bob said. The chief prosecutor bristled.

"That's just where you're wrong, Bub—it's little towns like McNeil that's the backbone of the country, and Hitler knows it."

Bob was stunned by the contextual force of the remark; he was silent.

During all of this heckling and crowding we were merely quiet and respectful. We didn't know that else to do. We learned then rapidly what we later learned about other provokers—including policemen—that almost always the tormentor is at a loss unless he can provoke a belligerent reaction as an excuse for further pressure or violence.

Every few minutes a car would come to a stop near us to spout out curious people. The news was getting around; later we discovered that towns five or ten miles away had begun to hear about the spies almost as soon as the group began to form around us. The people of Arkansas stood off and talked, nodding their heads and reading—with more interest than most poets can hope to arouse—George's blunderbuss of a poem.

Finally, to our great relief, the police car from Magnolia rolled up. A policeman was driving; a man in plain clothes, who turned out to be a federal revenue man, was beside him. The policeman gave us the first friendly word in a long time.

"That your work?" he asked Bob, nodding toward the picture still held by the evidence man. "That's pretty good."

The two representatives of the law took over, got our names, and gravely considered the indictments of the crowd. My letter was brought to light by the surrounding chorus of guards. The revenue man read it carefully, the onlookers craning over his shoulder. He retired to a new group. They read it. The officers took my camera, which had been confiscated by our guards, for evidence. They took *Leaves of Grass*. The policeman came back to the car, where we were standing.

He was the first man we had seen in a long time who didn't either stare at the ground when looked at or glare back.

The revenue man circulated around through the crowd for at least half an hour, talking to local leaders. The mob at its greatest numbered not more than sixty, or possibly seventy-five. All assurances given, the revenuer came back to the car; and our two rescuers—our captors in the eyes of the mob—whisked us back to camp, where we created a sensation as we rode down past the barracks in the police car.

The mob scene was over; our possessions were returned to us—except for the picture, the poem, and my letter, which were placed on exhibit at the Magnolia police station to satisfy inquirers that all precautions were being taken. At camp we doubled the night watch, for fear of trouble; but nothing happened.

And the next morning, before work, we three stood before the assembled campers—about one hundred men, clothed in various shades of denim and of bits from the ragbag, and seated on long wooden benches—and gave our version of what had happened, in order to quiet rumors and to help everyone learn from our experience. The argument about poetry got a big laugh, as did Bob's "Why, sir!" Before leaving that barracks hall we had to talk over the mobbing thoroughly; for it signified a problem we had to solve: When are men dangerous? How could we survive in our little society within a society? What could we do?

For that occasion, our camp director, a slow-talking preacher of the way of life taught by Jesus Christ, gave us the final word:

"I know you men think the scene was funny, in spite of its danger; and I suppose there's no harm in having fun out of it; but don't think that our neighbors here in Arkansas are hicks just because they see you as spies and dangerous men. Just remember that our government is spending millions of dollars and hiring the smartest men in the country to devote themselves full-time just to make everyone act that way."

We remembered, and set out to drain more swamps and put sod in more gullies in Arkansas.

Citizen Here on Earth

Selections from the Daily Writings, 1951–1993

Citizen Here on Earth

21 February 1951
To hold the voice down and the eyes up when facing someone who antagonizes you is a slight weight—once. But in a
lifetime it adds up to tons.

3 June 1953
The underground, peacetime underground, is essential for
the health, not of the state, but of the people.

16 August 1955
I belong to a small fanatical sect. We believe that current
ways of carrying on world affairs are malignant. We believe
that armies, and the kind of international dealings based on
armed might, will be self-perpetuating to a certain point—
and that that point may bring annihilation. Armies are a
result of obsolete ways—just as gibbets are, and as thumb-
screws are, and leper windows.

It might be that military appropriations should be increased. We need an easy, enlightened, well-paid, courteously
treated army—one so good that it will cooperate in its own
decline.

2 September 1957

The leaders of one country found their people attacking another country: that was a disaster of statesmanship, to lose their people like that.

In a second country the leaders found their country attacked. The people, though, had behaved with restraint, a triumph of statesmanship, and a condition very hard to achieve.

19 May 1963

One must learn to waver.

20 July 1964

In politics—and maybe elsewhere—I have assumed that one chooses when he can the person or policy he thinks best, regardless of how others choose. Now I begin to realize that many choose with much else in mind, such as—will this build the party? Can this choice get enough *others* as backing to be effective?

I have also spent my vote often in order to be a certain principled minority: there are people everywhere who won't kill, or who won't vote for a person—no matter the other reasons—who advocates or who has done this or that, etc. In taking such a role, part of my reason is that I *want* leaders to know there are such people in the public (and of course there *are:* could it be that we can become *beings* for whom genocide just is not tolerable? Isn't that the *kind* of being our international laws assume? If not, why is there a limit on *any* national policy?). In taking these positions I am of course aware of some of the hazards. But I want to raise the question of whether in society one takes his part guided by policy. Should one ever *be himself,* and let policy derive from a resolution of everyone's naive directness?

22 February 1966
A: I fear and dislike the regime in X.
B: If there were people working to be friendly there, would you like it better?
A: Yes, but there aren't any, or many, or they're ineffectual.
B: You are sure?
A: Yes.
B: In other words, if there were any, you would know?
A: Yes.
B: In our country I am friendly to them, and I count my existence as part of what mollifies them; they know and react about me by those infallible means you count on to inform you.

4 April 1966
One should talk to *people,* not to "nations," or "classes," or "professions," etc.

5 August 1966
Man's attention and power to relate: he can name and thus hold for attention anything; the choice of such things, along with other influences, makes literature. A person might just go around saying one word, and that word might turn into a slogan or reminder or indictment, e.g., "Hiroshima," "Geronimo."

31 October 1966

The question, "Wouldn't you fight for your country?" begs the real question, which is, "What is the best way to behave here and now to serve your country?" So one answer would be, "If it was the right thing to do, I would fight for my country. Now let's talk about what is the right thing to do." Or, "Wouldn't you refuse to fight if asked under wrong conditions to do so, for the sake of your country? So let's talk about *what to do* for our country."

19 July 1967

Arrows punish a bow.

22 August 1967

Children of heroes have glory for breakfast.

22 August 1967

You see trends you abhor but cannot prevent. You have always been told—and have believed—that citizens of a country are responsible for what happens there. Now you are on the spot. Many I know face this situation. They talk themselves, or especially their children, into being culture kamikazes.

22 September 1967

Those who champion democracy, but also make a fetish of never accepting anything they don't agree with—what advantage do they see in democracy?

22 November 1967

I must help anyone not plan a war.

23 November 1967

A job: To help make it possible for others to feel they can use pleasant methods to save the world. To influence *foreign* governments. To spring off little pieces of insight and save them, out of gross events and scenes.

22 March 1968

The Fallacy of Retrospective Certainty: People can select in the past certain events or persons and ascribe to them a crucial role in what eventuated. Sighting back past a chain of occurrences, one can say, "If someone had done this, then what followed could have been improved thus. Why didn't they act this way?" And sometimes the conclusion is, "Why don't I act that way, now?"

"I would have killed Hitler," they say, meaning, "I believe in assassination under some circumstances." A question: "What person would you assassinate now?" And if their principle is pushed to the further extreme they can be made remiss if they are not killing a succession of (retrospectively certain) troublemakers. But of course in actual life killing is not practiced or believed in by balanced people who realize the difficulties of judging consequences: it seems better to be civilized, to rely on group realizations, to cultivate order.

9 April 1968

Can injustice one way be corrected without the interim reaction that tries to impose injustice the other way?

13 May 1968

My country is No Man's Land.

9 October 1968
What the locomotive says, the whole train does.

29 October 1968
The people we found alien in the 1940s—pressing for victory, setting up the cold war, developing the bomb, strengthening the West—have turned against the war in Vietnam and have increased attempts to achieve "social justice." This change, though, is motivated and marked by much that still separates us: 1) aggression is a means of attaining the ends; 2) the machinations of certain evil persons must be stopped; 3) distrust, punishment, stern behavior is essential.

22 June 1969
Is it possible to be a pacifist if you think war is inevitable? I think it is likely. But I am a pacifist to postpone it, shorten it, de-escalate it. I do not think militarists make wars, or stop wars. People do.

25 September 1969
Every thought reorders the universe.

25 September 1969
Tyrants depend on helpers.

4 December 1969
When someone challenges you about a stand on social or political issues, you really are called upon to answer two things, one easy and one more difficult: 1) Your own position—this is easy and definite. 2) But also you feel it necessary to show

the relevance and effectiveness of your stand—this part can be extremely complex if your questioner occupies a position much different from yours. It is almost as difficult as converting someone in religion.

16 January 1970
Does our readiness for violence and confrontation in literature have cumulative effect in our lives?

21 April 1970
When there is a way to win, the enemy are dead.

8 April 1970
Opening Statement: Conference on Poetry and the National Conscience, University of Maryland
Poetry and other arts come from acceptance of little signals that immediate experience contributes to beings who are alive and fallible, and changing. Any conscience relevant to that kind of activity will tend to be un-national, not American or foreign, or North or South, or Black or White, or East—but alive and ready to confer.

22 August 1970
Seeing one side at a time, we blunder. Truth has no perspective.

16 September 1970
My tremors are small, perhaps unmeaning, but like Galileo I can go away muttering, "Still, it moves."

18 November 1970
Some butter is harder than other, but none can challenge the knife.

25 November 1970
When a war looms, the enemy emerges as wrong and a menace. How long before was it wrong and a menace? What was done then? Should more have been done earlier? Could it have been swayed earlier? Were the aggressive people now among those trying to sway earlier?

3 July 1971
Every war has two losers.

11 September 1971
People rebelling against what they feel brought on World War II are re-enacting that time.

23 June 1973
You are rich by how far a battle is.

13 August 1974
A speech is something you say so as to distract attention from what you do not say.

20 September 1974
One trouble about language is that people sometimes believe what you say, and you were only trying it out.

16 November 1974
You wanted too much in this world and now it has hurt you; you condemn it by condemning its people.

17 October 1974
What really sets a car off right is a good driver.

1 December 1974
Divisions among groups bring forward aggressive leaders, whose function requires of them an emphasizing of positive qualities in their own group, a tolerance of distortion in regard to the "enemy," a temporary using of means ordinarily frowned upon. War leaders are liars.

10 December 1974
When I feel brave I know I'm afraid.

1 February 1975
Sure, there is darkness in the world, but when I want to read I use the light.

14 May 1975
People relate to what other people see and relate to. But back of all that is a day, an ideal place, a location to face toward always. It is other than *people*. Somewhere out there is Mecca.

6 August 1975
Two cultures surround us. One assumes that short-term evasions for long-term goods will prevail: selling, promoting, elocution, patriotism, orthodoxy, forensics, officialism—these characterize that culture.

The other relies on some kind of human immediacy and long-term rationale: professionalism, counseling, personal allegiances, quick perceptions, freedom—these characterize the second culture.

Any artist lives by the second.

Writers, teachers, friends obviously ally themselves with the second. Any authoritarian regime links to the first.

17 October 1975
You are part of what you criticize, or you don't know enough about it to criticize.

28 October 1975
Above a head that is orating I glimpse a sign.

19 February 1976
Beat your megaphones into ear trumpets.

4 July 1976
Ambition: Something utterly fair to everybody.

30 October 1976
If you'll be someone else, I will.

13 December 1976
It helps to know as soon as possible when you have lost, or won.

23 July 1977
Last night I dreamed the "other" side needed a part for its
war machine, and we were tossing it to them, but they kept
being unable to catch.

31 July 1977
It took me no trouble at all to find and seek out the story
of this apparently ordinary old person:

"You would think from the way I live that my life has
always been usual, and it is true that I consider myself common, but without trying I can recount to you actual events
in my life that will sound like extreme and sensational parts
of the plight of modern man.

"I was captured, for instance, in the early stages of the
war of 1941, and I spent three years as a prisoner. If you died,
you died—and I have no way to report on such prisoners; but
if you lived you certainly received a living diet—remember
that. And our only source on life in the camps is from survivors. I was one."

5 May 1978
Why does demonstration, assertiveness, parading, etc.,
disquiet me? Partly because democratic choice implies not
only freedom for the individual but *value* from what the individual brings to the consensus. If public action creates turbulence, intimidation, distortion of the frequency and
distribution of more quietly held views, then *individual*
thought is damaged both in its occurrence and in its expres-
sion. I think that quiet individual decision should count:
public conduct should encourage it, not put it in hazard.

3 July 1978
Some people are secure only when they win.

28 August 1978
If you like a country, it's yours. Disliked, it belongs to somebody else.

11 October 1978
Living traditionally, the country life, we cultivate the ground. We know the seed will produce after its kind. Why then do we sow suspicion and hatred in some places? If we show goodwill, honesty, reliability, industry, thrift, cheer, will these tend to produce those qualities in others around us? And the contrary is true too?

But do we have enemies? Whence came their feelings toward us? Can a serenity view and understand?

1 November 1978
One of the consistent impulses of my life is to reduce uncertainties. But I find myself disquieted by expressions of certainty, or even by the manner of those who give off the sense of relying on their distinctive possession of truth.

At any given moment, even a cloud is certain.

17 April 1979
Are there any differences among people? Yes. Then even in enemy nations there are differences in how firm the "enemy" feelings are? Yes. Does this make any difference in your reactions? Well.

1 May 1979

"Some people are idealists: they keep leaning to make the world different. They should face up to the way things are, and accept them."

"Well, my leg is broken—I guess I'll just like that strange angle my leg has as it lies there."

18 May 1979

Stafford's Gettysburg Address: These dead people were brave.

21 September 1979

Dream: One country kept sending doves flying over another, but were forced to stop. One dove, though, was already in the air.

22 October 1979

Try these:

Lying is wrong, between equals.

Save the world by torturing one innocent child? Which innocent child?

22 October 1979

If you were smart enough it wouldn't make any difference if someone were lying. In fact, human concern about honesty would seem to you just quaint. There would be many other considerations you would see as more important—perception, vigor, sociability.

Think of two people you can be with:

One is dishonest, friendly, clean, respectful, loving; the other is honest, unfriendly, dirty, disrespectful, arrogant, spiteful.

5 November 1979
Why are there *nations* you don't like? That is a fiction you are responding to—a label put onto millions of varied individuals. Your feeling has been created, and created by interests you might do well to analyze.

11 November 1979
The Militarist's Farewell: Good-bye, Boomerang, see you later.

6 January 1980
Some people want justice. They like to stand in the rain and think about a roof that would shelter them if only . . . — you supply the rest. It can be anything, just so it isn't true.

5 March 1980
Are we sort of hostages, to "enemy" nations? And are "enemy" populaces sort of hostages to our military? If certain things happen, we will be bombed. And if certain other things happen, they will. Mutual hostages, held under guns.

2 April 1980
Our "leaders" viewed as entertainers: Their drama becomes more important than the essential qualities of leadership. Our artists too are entertainers and succeed in large part by qualities so related. We do not learn, but are reminded, stroked.

13 May 1980
A democracy may fail to gain participation from nonassertive people. If you want a system that allows active roles for activists, that's one thing; if your objective is to gain from the

insights of all citizens, that's a different thing. The creative life of unknown people might be a tremendous hidden river. An intelligent leader might want, not just the complaints and declamatory input, but the tide of quiet perceptions from everywhere in the populace; might promote an incessant quizzing of all minds. Contribution of opinion might be more than a right—it might be a need, a salvation, and not just for the individual but for the society. And the individual might react in a democracy in light of whether in fact opinions are sought or just tolerated: if a contribution isn't worthy in terms of the welfare of the group, the individual might not be all that eager to insist on it.

15 May 1980
In the world these days a habit has come to dominate—the habit of the state. For security, for control of environment, for life-planning, . . . we rely on a social organism that is world-powerful. No animal, no individual, very few germs can hold out against the attention and intentions of the state. It promotes itself—education, rivalry with other states, mock and real elections, regulation and hence coverage with news. . . . A stateless individual can't move or get a job or be "protected."

31 May 1980
Right after the war we liked green.

25 June 1980
Most problems I solve by going away.

30 July 1980
Burden of what is not said. Our cherished refraining from speech. Fields where no stones are. Undeclared peace.

3 September 1980
Dream: A box labeled: "Sorry. War."

11 September 1980
In the sagas, those who lost shouldn't have resisted.

11 September 1980
Being wrong is easy. *How* to be when wrong is harder.

14 September 1980
The bitter knowledge that you have been stupidly winning.

12 October 1980
You are coming toward history all the time and you keep zigzagging but it always turns out to be there waiting, and—clunk—you arrive again and again.

24 October 1980
If you like a soft answer do you have to sacrifice honesty?

29 November 1980
When you get far enough away for perspective, one of the aspects of the world is its quiet. Occasions for such realization occur to me, like, "From far enough away, even a war is a murmur."

3 December 1980

Remember—some doves try harder than other doves and some serpents are pretty dumb.

20 December 1980

The dread of things that you know have already been—why that? These things are throughout history, and not the deeds of anyone you know or are likely to know. Such will happen again. Maybe to you and to people you know. You can be caught up emotionally, even to frenzy. Can you do anything rational, now? The UN is one channel. FOR [Fellowship of Reconciliation] is another. Your government? Yes, in some of its actions. And in your own daily actions.

1 July 1981

To a successful, bustling, triumphant accomplisher: "What's your problem?"

11 July 1981

A place back of this fort, now filled with flowers, hollowed in rock for a bunker, shelters a fawn.

12 July 1981

You can't help noticing these days that right hasn't prevailed.

14 July 1981

Two democracies: One where you have a right to speak, another where you maximize what you hear.

Two censorships: One where the law prohibits utterance,

another where strong characters dominate and prevent real interchange.

"I really told them off." "I really listened better than they did."

Those times you caught them out and showed them up—they learned how stupid they are. But now you'll never hear the little song of their purring throats, and you'll never know what they think, when you say hello.

11 August 1981
If I resent someone's arrogance, is it because I have that competitive quality from which arrogance comes?

4 September 1981
Not just the doing of justice, but the realization of the doing of justice, is the job. The *feeling* of justice is a good feeling; the measuring of it is difficult verging on impossible. In law maybe not enough is done about cultivating that feeling.

12 September 1981
"Oracle, where will I begin to be saved?"
Here.
"When do the proofs come?"
Now.
"Who can bring this about?"
You.
"Is there ever anyone else to help?"
No.
"What happens to people who hurt me?"
It's cold where they live.

"Do they die?"

Yes.

12 September 1981

The wind you walk against but do not feel is ignorance. Your foolish face has happiness on one side, but the world pressed on the other.

16 September 1981

Winners can lose what winning was for.

20 October 1981

A clear realization about battle unfits a soldier.

The eye that can stand the sun can't see in shadow.

Some questions you would ask of God prove you unfit for God's company.

The root and the flower have to trust each other.

Other parts of the car can say maybe, but the battery has to say yes.

2 December 1981

Consciousness isn't so much. I liked it better before I woke up, even though my dream terrified me: it was a first day of war, and everyone (living in a kind of hospital or hotel) was concentrated on imminent triumph. Well, a few had furtive thoughts, and books they kept referring to. And some were marked by a difference, sort of a different look, or collar. By day's end casualties began to come in—and then the report of *losing*. Those *different* people slunk here and there, and I knew a saying: "The losing are merciless."

4 December 1981
Was there ever anyone who understood the anguish of still
being subject to allegiances you have begun to distrust?
Nietzsche did.

10 December 1981
Forceful speaker: The bow was all right, but the arrows
weren't any good.

12 December 1981
All the while, back of the apparent scenario there is the real
scenario; and our fears and appetites are serving some cause.
What is the opposite of paranoia?

17 December 1981
My plan is, to be scared.

16 February 1982
My belief is what my whole life says.

17 February 1982
If my enemies are strong and right, are they enemies?
And if they are mistaken, should I work to help them?

17 February 1982
More things are true than are worth saying.
"What I said was the truth." "But why did you say it?"

19 February 1982
Is it all right if we talk?
OK. Is it all right if we disagree?
OK. Then is it all right if you lose?

19 February 1982
In that war we persuaded ourselves that the people we were
killing were really bad.

4 March 1982
Between roars the lion purrs.

1 May 1982
A Response for Those Who Told Us How Dumb We Were: You
think we didn't know?

27 May 1982
Where the knife is when it cuts is my kind of tradition.

30 May 1982
I woke up thinking, "History may try again."

26 June 1982
We survive by our limitations.

8 July 1982
Epic: A sustained account of evils of our time.

15 August 1982

The world and its events are out there—various, surprising, athletic in possibility—and the addicts of the fumes of belief bend over their little private glow, lost in their delusions of psychic omnipotence.

20 August 1982

A champion is just someone who hasn't met a live lion.

1 October 1982

Places where history happened—they mark these, where you stop and imagine how you got here.

You come back to a place and be different, but you can't forget. You turn away from any hero—the study of motives has complicated these battlefields, and looking back is a different perspective. I look forward, but the rearview mirror unreels all the reasons for traveling, and where I was gets little.

11 October 1982

Many questions: Is it better to be a big country, or a little country? Is it better to be safe by being strong, or by being friends?

14 October 1982

I don't like to hear from victims. At one remove they remind of oppressors. And I don't like oppressors. Oppressors have become the way they are through damaging conditions. Like victims. I want to turn and start over again. As for myself, I don't want to be an oppressor, nor be like a victim.

There are probably ways to live so as to shut out chances to be victimized. Those ways are probably worse than being a victim.

22 November 1982
The sickness of lusting after justice.

22 November 1982
Do I respect others to the degree that I fear them?

4 January 1983
If it should happen you wake up and Armageddon has come, lie still.

29 January 1983
Maybe our needs are deeper than our appetites.

23 February 1983
Frogs keep trying to say it right. Truth is a stutter.

1 March 1983
In the cold I will wander, in caves build a fire and wait— where are the soldiers who promised their army would survive the winter? Only the wind has never forsaken us. It comes bearing its knife, true till death.

5 May 1983
Intentions have side effects.

4 July 1983

In the war some of the enemy didn't fight very hard, and some of us didn't either. Between battles unregarded peace crept in while warriors were sleeping.

28 October 1983

Hearing the president: The question is not whether foreign nations engage in unfriendly acts. The question is why they engage in unfriendly acts toward us, and whether we can act so as to reduce that enmity. We can make enemies and then be brave: are there other ways?

31 October 1983

You may win a war you are sorry to have started.

28 November 1983

In some rooms a sound is harsh: echoes, clashing reverberations, a flat, repeating effect—these multiply any original sound. There are people like those rooms: an event in their company echoes, clashes, repeats. If it's a bad event, it goes on and on. Some other people are the opposite: they are good to be with in bad times. It is not just extremes that mark those clashing companions. Every little encounter gives off either garish overtones or mellow ones.

15 December 1983

Kinds of statements: An assessment, judgment, opinion that derives from experience not sufficient to validate it, like, "Mine is the best . . ." from someone who has not surveyed the field. Or, "We will never . . ." by someone not in control of "we." Or, "The United States stands . . ."

16 December 1983

Another way around: If a nation's policy is criminal, we demand that citizens refuse to go along. There is a gradient of acceptance for a good citizen: one should accept up to a degree, but beyond that should refuse. As that gradient approaches the critical point people begin to feel the anguish that is near to being decisive. In purely political discussions that gradient is usually ignored.

The presence of enemies who approximate one's conduct relieves that anguish, but a perception that such enemies are being created partly by one's own conduct reduces that relief. So we tend to avoid that perception, and in order to do so we get habits of evasion. Such evasions are the inherent or inner evil. Finally, to live with that evil we "damage, you might say, the ear's innermost chamber where we hear the heavy noise of the dragon's tail moving over the dead leaves."—John Cheever, *Characters That Will Not Appear*

27 December 1983

Some of the impulses and actions we regret result from qualities we have to possess in order to live.

3 February 1984

Sometimes you would rather do something wrong than do nothing: you have waited for change, and you see it won't happen, and there has to be some, sooner or later—and then maybe you can act helpfully. So—you nudge the dangerous, balanced confusion, and it falls with a clatter.

15 February 1984

Maybe so long as people try for something for nothing there will be crime and war.

16 February 1984

Because you cheered when the moon rose, you have received secret absolution: when they march you away someone will look back. In this world, that's redemption.

21 March 1984

I live in a foreign country.

5 April 1984

The job of an army requires what the nature of a soldier becomes. And soldiers vote.

A country enters that swirl—and may win too many wars.

19 April 1984

My country says it guarantees rights, but the world I come from is much more enigmatic than that.

20 April 1984

A book: Explaining the day-by-day existence of someone in a country that gradually moves toward tyranny, toward terrorizing the world. Each step helps create the pressure from abroad that justifies the next step.

22 April 1984

Willows don't have any heroes.

25 April 1984
Stars are a sanctuary: after politics one looks for science, a cool retreat.

25 April 1984
Winners in a game like that are unforgivable. In some games it is important to lose.

24 May 1984
The incapacitating excitement of battle overcame me, the surge of commitment, the love of our soldiers—their foolish bravery. The warm bias of friendship caught my judgment and bent it toward all the fallible loyalties. When it was evening at home I lost balance; I loved whatever was ours. Only when it was past, when the wars and loves and families were gone, did I perceive cold, clear outlines and how equal were friends and enemies. A new light came to me, and I rejoiced in the weakness, the flaws—even the evil—that appeared in the bright bright scenes my neutrality began to discover all around me.

27 June 1984
Storms happen. One goes. One comes. Between, we midges dance in the sun.

29 June 1984
Mistakes you make are guides for where to go; snowflakes the storm brings are shelter from its cold.

6 July 1984
It dawns on us, the last people, that the world will survive us.

28 July 1984

Half-dream last night—the unthinkable: the good thing about our adversary is that it is always bad; even when it seems to be good it has other motives. (We used to say "Our Enemy," but that created problems when brief periods of good feeling would call the term in question. More about this later.)

By now we have so frightful a deterrence—and they have—that we are—relatively—safe from war, even if miscalculation comes. (More on that later.) But there is another exception: what if they don't believe we will use our atomic weapons? We must convince them that we will, and on occasion we must appear crazy enough to do so. And they must do the same.

But we don't *really* dare resort to the atomic option, so we must have convincing and poised other weapons, too, in case a war comes in which we wouldn't want to be the first to use the ultimate terror (but we *might,* remember).

An insidious danger would be that the Adversary would begin to act friendly and thus lull us into lapsing our readiness—a window of vulnerability would come, a missile gap, or a tank gap, or a boat gap (these are especially troublesome gaps—the missile gap would hardly make any difference, because what's left wouldn't have any people to appreciate it).

There's a whole unthinkable other set of problems: what our *friends* might do to us. It is notorious that other countries are lazy about who they let get into power. What happens if they decide they are chosen for glory, not sometime, but now? . . .

And yet another nightmare: what if even in this country, the deterrent falls under control of people we don't trust?

Or what if our counterespionage service goes counter-counter?

The lowest-down trick would be if our adversary acted so nice to us that we'd forget how bad they are. And we'd get to liking them, despite their past and their present fakery.

We must be on our guard, especially when it seems we shouldn't. But other times too.

2 August 1984
Why worry about me—I'm just part of the program. Mistakes I make will become history, which is instructive if you survive it, and exemplary if you don't.

18 August 1984
Twenty years ago or so it began to dawn on me how weak and fallible people are, how habits and limited environments had fostered institutionalized smugness and vainglory: when saber-toothed tigers died out bravery began to be possible; lack of association with superior sensibilities allows the assumption that we apprehend all that is around us; success at customary activities enables us to assume that we are in control of anything we put our minds to. This mirror that we admire will shatter if touched by any of the real rocks around us.

8 November 1984
Unsmiling, the economist presents the budget needed for defense. We smile: that sum is the whole cost of what we defend.

Thus moving all things, we return to point zero.

It is cold out here on this point, and we scramble for something else. Maybe discourage the enemy, instead of defend?

At least we might hope our advisor would smile.

19 November 1984
My work is the only independence I have—or reveal.

29 November 1984
Dream: I am in an army and we are in a place like a stadium and are supposed to start fighting; but we look at each other and somehow just don't quite get started. Then we realize that maybe we won't have the war. I am aware of the chancy nature of things—if we can keep from frightening each other, maybe it all won't start.

9 December 1984
Gradually it begins to get to you: what they want to say overloads the air, and your small voice is neglected. You think about their words and what is behind them. Gradually you separate interest from accomplishment, but still the effect of being only a receiver chokes you.

In tunnels where they hid during bombings the Welsh would sing. No one outside could hear them. Their songs never silenced a plane. But in that rich darkness their music sounded so pure that a diamond formed in the soul.

13 January 1985
Social leverages:
Simple threat—dangerous mostly to the threatener, for society won't tolerate overt performance. But as a bluff it works.

Flattery—useful over and over, plain, disguised.
Righteousness—wielded in myriads of ways by individuals
and institutions.
High-ground benevolence—powerful and persuasive; the
main leverage used by parents and other well-positioned
people.

18 January 1985
Taking a position; observing; remarking—that's a way to be.
Another way is not taking a position; following; changing.
Some people live by the first.
Mostly I think I favor the second, maybe (the maybe puts me
into that second person, I think).
The first tends to be an adversary, using a scales not balanced.

22 February 1985
The scar here on my cheek is 1942, a long year. It is what our
country is now about. Creating the emergencies that justify
emergency action.

31 March 1985
The wars we haven't had saved many lives.

12 April 1985
Beyond inlets from the sea, a slow upsurging tide of green—
the forest. It fingers forth from gravel, levering out persis-
tently. The tide doesn't stop at the shore, but streams inland
in tiny threads, to rise by stealth. And the forest waves.
It guides us north to the heart country where no whisper
comes of the sun.

Restless after the tide, kelp strains toward dark. All direction wavers: we know that our knowledge obscures whatever comes new. Kelp turns because what pulls doesn't turn.

If the professor can forget New London and the submarines, forget how that tide invents itself to come back after it disappears, then a library can ride on the back of the hostages. And all the serene facts can sleep their linear uses. Part of the wrong dream, we pass New London where the *Nautilus,* a stately mansion, slips out into darkness. Hostages, we wait. A convention (procession) of linear fact registers on the screen and the *Nautilus*—maybe a mistake—lowers and glides into its mothering ambush, then darkens toward destiny.

Bright as a tiger, the *Nautilus* leans down. Darkness is where it will hide. People send it where it will go, to be ready to give what they will receive. An adequate power, they say, to carry its message: what people give, what people will receive. An array of linear fact, a truly generous return.

The image of America—delivered by people who live in big centers—is being drawn by people who are not where the face is.

9 May 1985
Certain threads will stretch a long way, become tangled, hardly noticed. But never be broken.

31 July 1985
Our world is a deluge of news. "Information" drowns us, and what we need to know or to keep in mind gets lost, not through repression by authority but by our own inability to sort out what comes at us, and to link parts to their pattern of significance.

Some news ought to be repeated, reminded, headlined often; and just as a truck backing up on a job has a repeating horn, so an alarm needs to sound—not that it's news when a truck backs up, but that it continues to be a danger when it does so.

7 August 1985
Fierce people are scared.

27 August 1985
Biters from fear. Many people, even the fiercest, are that. Many disruptive. Many purposefully careless. Many a panicky kitten scratches.

22 October 1985
A person crawls. Proud people have hands and knees.

4 December 1985
Those rewarded by leaders, and the leaders themselves: they like each other very much.

11 December 1985
Whenever you were born you could have been somebody else, and in another time and place. So part of your attention goes to changing yourself, and looking around. Later you re-alize that you are the right person to be you, and that other places are a distraction from important things.

It happened that the important people you met had missed certain events you found essential; therefore the world never caught up. These leaders were distracted with money when part of the world blew away through Kansas in the 30s. They were occupied in Europe and Asia when someone noticed the trees were dying in the 40s. A person found out language had fooled us for centuries, and these leaders didn't hear about it but went on in the old way.

3 January 1986
Whoso teases the lion saves up some drama.

31 January 1986
On a battlefield the flies don't care who wins.

20 March 1986
Your country is invading a distant land.

11 April 1986
Fool that I am, I keep thinking things will work out, that we can coast along while injustice prevails, and somehow it will change.

2 May 1986
Do not be surprised if things go wrong—mistakes in the past have their consequences, and what we have been does not just disappear through good intentions now. If evil could be canceled at once by a good act, it would not be very evil.

7 May 1986
Human beings do not deserve firm opinions on certain important issues. Religion, for instance—the firmly religious believers and the firmly denying unbelievers are alike too positive. And about nations—it is notorious that nationalistic postures go with the chances of residency. Apparently

"great leaders" are in the nature of things distorted in intellect so as to occupy firm positions on matters that intellectuals perceive as problematical.

6 July 1986

A person says, "I'm resigning from the human race. They are as Swift said the most miserable, odious race of vermin ever to inhabit the earth."

Immediately it is apparent that this person is wrong somehow. Not knowing all people, one can't reasonably sweep them all aside. And whatever grounds for judgment are used, they are based on *human* perception and feeling. Besides, so sweeping an assessment is on the face of it a mark of imbalance and sickness.

But wait—many people choose a whole nation and make such an assessment: The idea that Nazi Germany was monolithic, and that anyone there who claimed virtue while the war years went on is dishonest. The judgment that any Russian who says something sympathetic is a secret agent. . . .

3 August 1986

Most revolutionists are too frivolous about violence and sacrifice, and *winning*. They are not serious enough to stay on a track, to *guide* a revolution. They are hobbyists.

13 September 1986

Odd: You say once the U.S. has a decided edge its enemies will have to accede to accommodation. And you say the enemies have the edge now. . . .

21 November 1986
Many today perceive that a government, in order to lead, must establish credibility. It must cultivate a majority. It must put a good face on what it is doing. Such a government, presumably, is trying to influence the people. Well, I am not one of the leaders. I am one of the people. And I am not scrambling to establish that credibility—I am judging it. And as for the "good face," I am assessing whether it is just a face.

13 December 1986
You let one uniform salute another, and the last start the war. It stops when the little ones turn away from the big one. No more saluting.

25 December 1986
The world as it is does contain flint and the spark hidden till struck, occasional wind that somewhere everlastingly rushes across all that it left before. Also, a turn in thought may cancel evil by grace when without knowing we stumble on boulders that later turn out to be gold. A vine we had began to change color; some element in its hunger discovered another island beyond autumn and reached for it.

28 December 1986
Which country will the U.S. invade this year?

30 December 1986
A quirk in what "the truth" is: In national affairs, leaders may assess prospects a certain way, really; but they voice only those opinions that will keep the fickle, fallible populace on

the right track, so as to prevent oscillations of public opinion from troubling the carrying on of policy. "Don't arouse undue expectations."

1 February 1987
The bow when strung sings of equality, wilderness generous and starting all over again. The arrow mentioned sincerity: "I'll go where you say."

5 June 1987
Some people are blinded by their experience. Soldiers know how important war is. Owners of slaves learn every day how inferior subject peoples are.

13 June 1987
If your enemy is an unjust person, why do you think that proof of injustice will bring about a change?

15 June 1987
Lightning flashes still flicker on the horizon, faint but there. I predict a storm waiting for a reason.

15 June 1987
To know, to be convinced, is not at once to understand, or to bring into an individual's life the sustained adjustment to a new presence. Maybe it is unsustainable, or at least we had learned to live with [the new presence], adjusting to its caprices by plans for surviving uncertainties and by intricate beliefs that grew and accompanied us. But certain investigators began to suspect a background of all the world of the senses, a background that could be manipulated; and the

rest of the world, by lurid, convincing demonstration in the 1940s, came to believe.

That demonstration by destruction carried a promise, also: the aim and control of that power. Only cumulative efforts can approach it. And perhaps what is found can become a part of the life we all share.

17 June 1987
Somebody told me there used to be a law,
if you don't believe in it, don't obey the law.
Hard to enforce, uncertain except in war
when winners need reasons for what they have to do.

17 June 1987
The new and cumulative ability to manipulate the world around us may dazzle our senses. And what we do with our lives in the presence of such opportunities may be neglected.

24 July 1987
Dream: With maybe a dozen others I am a prisoner in Iran. We know we are hostages and that our future depends on what happens between our countries. There is a house where we are held; we can look at a street below us.

30 July 1987
Success may not mean you did right.

15 August 1987
There are people so deeply persuaded of the value of their preferences that those preferences become priorities for any

group, because reiteration overcomes any balancing of preferences of other people: these deeply persuaded people are called "leaders."

22 August 1987
Today in society you need a tendency not to believe.

29 September 1987
Citizens feel they represent their country, that they identify with what it does. The individual, though, is riding a tiger. To guide one's country is like guiding a tornado.

10 November 1987
Strange, but life isn't serious anymore. Oh, people get incensed about issues, about atrocities that flare in the news, about the long, grinding subjugation of women. We are alert for such topics. But the more we perceive, the more we destroy our sense of the immediate value of living. Now we tell each other that death is better than oppression. Then, we value life too much for such frivolous opinions.

Today popular magazines pour consumer solaces endlessly, but their articles and stories are about lives that are shallow, desperate, banal, blighted. And the public wander from one distraction to another, carrying their emptiness within them: "I acquiesce in the deterrent of terror. I am preserved by my readiness to kill them all."

29 November 1987
How far down the road are you looking? Where you turn off? Where a bridge waits? Into the fog?

22 January 1988
The arrow tells what the archer meant to say.

12 March 1988
All that happens in our time osmoses into our art: any war with its blend of aggression and fear and special kinds of "justice," for instance, will color all else.

17 May 1988
For a while, after a war, if you are stupid enough you could cheer. There isn't anything sweeter than a victory, and a good roof over your head, and a family, and being ignorant. But then your old buddies come around and say, "Let's go again, against anybody—there is always injustice." This time, though, it was different. You saw farther than the bullets went. You saw the end before it ended.

14 August 1988
In my dream it was like wartime, being afraid to speak out. Every day, everywhere, full of menace.

29 August 1988
Children playing with knives.
Children swearing. Children
running a country.

28 September 1988
Certain voices live on assumptions that the speakers think are conclusions. The state can't feel. It can't have our undivided loyalty, for the sources of its power and wisdom are capricious.

Meanwhile, Right wanders from person to person and some-times has to live in the open without shelter.

15 October 1988
There are a lot of berserk people in the world. But maybe that experience of being a CO was an abrupt lesson in the feeling that you are *in* but not *of* this nation.

27 June 1989
Is it peace when the rockets are aimed at each other?

1 October 1989
Many a road, sure of a destination, sets off and gets lost from a goal that even if found would be a mistake.

17 December 1989
If some recent atrocity cannot be forgotten, for to do for-getting is implicitly to condone it, then remote atrocities have just as much right to our attention. "We" are guilty of what "we" did to the Neanderthals. The righteous condone their shrillness by principles they choose arbitrarily. I observe them as phenomena, as evidence, as symptoms, but not as guides.

Nietzsche saw that the life preservers the righteous clutched were made of lead.

8 February 1990
Are some of the enemy better than others?

21 April 1990

People look at my books on Gandhi and say, "He didn't prevail against his enemies." These people didn't even consider that there might be some aim other than their idea of prevailing.

12 August 1990

"Your policy of reconciliation would work if people were good, but they are not." Response: *"Some of the people."*

19 August 1990

I felt like a mirror being carried through a crowd, not knowing what to reflect.

28 August 1990

You don't want to hurt your enemy. Unconvinced, I checked my knife again.

19 December 1990

In every generation's picture, if you had a gap for those who died young, think of the talents death deprived us of. Our notable are just the few, not perhaps the best, but just the chance remnant.

23 December 1990

The commander plans and decides, enjoying credit and creation; the soldier goes and does whatever he is told. In my dugout I wait for bombs or commands. Both hit the roof hard.

6 January 1991

In the center of human life are those who hold it together. They make home what it is. They listen to "leaders," receive, decide. Whatever country is, whatever a profession, a town— they establish that. "The center cannot hold"—well, they are that center. What we lament is not enough of these people, not an environment for them. "Nice guys finish last"—is it that kind of world?

Why do tears come in our eyes? We think about these people, the center. When they go, the center is weakened. It needs a certain quality to fill it, strengthen it. No use saying, "Let's take their place." We know we can't do that. Their going is absolute. It is a loss. Time did this to us. It erased them. And it isn't making people like them anymore.

20 January 1991

War prunes the tree, taking the best branches.

23 January 1991

When people get excited they get more sure of their opinions.

17 February 1991

At first the pen doesn't know where to go. It has been away awhile and is now a little aimless. Besides, one of the world wars has begun somewhere off there beyond the horizon, making any random journey seem frivolous or even an act of treason. ("What are you doing, Daddy, in that evident or more hidden war that is always going on whether you know it or not?")

So the pen, taking account of all that but unable still to do much about it, listens carefully to its own whispering and tries whatever direction the next word wants to go, meanwhile keeping in mind that sooner or later it will be necessary to spell out a meaning for all apparent meandering. (If you ever touch the real lost way you never even want to find your main path again; that's what bothers those who intend to guide you.) (What they're afraid of is, a new star shows up and all the old patterns turn into delusions and chaos.)

No wonder the pen tries to escape its past by pretending to have a future. There might be a way to escape, somewhere in the middle of things, if that awful responsibility of beginning and ending didn't haunt all who have to travel to live.

25 February 1991
Do I create hurt in the world? Could even my sympathy help create the appetite for it? Could people waked up to their feelings then suffer more? Maybe I should look away?

2 March 1991
Come, be human. Sit down and let's talk.

5 March 1991
Recently a new serenity has touched me, and a feeling of wisdom. No, this is not a proud feeling, a feeling of being in control, but an acceptance of not being in control.

10 March 1991
My bitter enemies: The rottener the teeth the worse the bite.

14 March 1991
Those who follow games loved the war. They didn't like
the killing. They wish that hadn't happened. But it was
necessary.

30 May 1991
By the power of instant vision all over the world, a battle
and its results have rolled past an audience fascinated and
shocked. Through the analytical insight of medicine, a populace has glimpsed that a chemical imbalance in its leader
brought catastrophe to hundreds of thousands across wide
seas. And similar imbalances in "the enemy" justified what
happened. All the arrangements worked, and the successful
war was over. But everyone senses that something awful happened that shouldn't have been permitted to happen.

14 July 1991
At what point does one's continued presence at a place become complicity in what happens there? Does moving to
another place remove the complicity? Does survival mean
complicity? Could there be a world in which survival means
complicity? Or would dying do that? Or being comfortable?

26 August 1991
In small things a person could be exemplary while perhaps in
one large thing absolutely to be condemned.

1 September 1991
Running your engine's revs up into the red zone won't
do any good, and becoming strident on an issue may be
counterproductive.

23 September 1991
In a dream last night—a whole different civilization, pastoral, quiet. (My cheerful self took over, soothed my world, made it what I needed.) My "mistakes" about the objective world are my salvation.

27 September 1991
The main damage of the war turns out to be the enmities: people can't work together, make deals, relax from war taxes, plan for sustained production, reconstruct ways of maintaining trust.

30 September 1991
Like a tree, like a leaf, some day to be nothing, after a war, after no one notices for years, to disappear, driven downward, maybe in snow, and its whispering: "Where are you, God? I have waited a long time, and fallen."

1 October 1991
The body you wear, its outline, the cut of its coat and skirt or pants, will go out of style. And the young, wearing their new, semi-permanent bodies, will try to forget history and how it comes clanking along like a tank no matter where they run, or how loud you laugh at the tank—damaged old bodies around you that used to be stylish.

One young statue fell after the war and weathered into a quaint old body that squinted sideways from the grass. They hauled it away quickly, lest the new heroes read their inscriptions and think about how heavy stone is at night or in the rain.

13 October 1991, In Vienna

For years these lined faces have told me how it was, and then said, with a shake of the head, "You don't understand." They look farther away and sigh. What they went through, in a war, in a depression, or when the city fell, has given them something. They pity those who lack these occasions for being pitied. "You will never know," they say. "You weren't there. I'm sorry, but there is no way [for you] to attain this knowledge I have." And they look off into that long corridor where heroes line up for their centuries of patient eminence.

"Did you see the massacres?" I ask. And they stare back at me:

"It wasn't like that."

"Was that the year of the potatoes?" I ask.

They lift their shoulders, they spread their hands. "You don't see it. You don't get the picture." They straighten their napkins and look out a window. What they see is an avenue only they and their kind, gifted by a certain pain, can have.

13 October 1991

Political leaders depend on having an electorate that will permit the right moves.

14 October 1991

Protest poetry—could there be consensus poetry?

15 October 1991

We talked about protest—my WWII protest, for instance—but then we went back to *before* the war, race relations. In general, I think they assume the high ground and thus avoid assessing real alternatives.

19 October 1991

In our society one trend is toward confrontation, vulgarity; another trend is toward social action against some of the results of vulgarity (prejudice, bullying, harassment). Confused people entangle themselves in both.

20 October 1991

Several generations now have lived by values or disvalues generated by war, including the Cold War and its reliance on "deterrence" through terror. The situation continues the social qualities of confrontation, competition, power; and we now have a world balanced continually on the brink. Brinkmanship is our current unnoticed religion or prevailing myth.

23 October 1991

Question: Do big dogs have more importance than little dogs? And people? Do loud sounds mean more than soft sounds? On the street? In music? At night? In a talk? They call some people "great" and make their monuments large. What does this show about where our allegiances turn? Why are churches tall?

28 October 1991

You like the moon but you wouldn't want it in your house or any bigger.

1 November 1991

Everyone is a conscientious objector to something. Are there things you wouldn't do? Well.

27 November 1991
Why was I given citizenship here on Earth?

28 November 1991
People who react randomly, angrily, with odd surges of negativity, have a disability that should be cared for just as generously as other disabilities. Their thinking is a hobble. Their seizures paralyze their ability to perceive. They stumble from one mistake to another.

30 November 1991
My preference for lies isn't just for my own—I like other people's lies too. History is the lies people have agreed on?

17 January 1992
Blaming others: I do my evil in different ways.

2 March 1992
Two stances toward my life:
1. My way of existing can control what happens. If I am brave, if I confront things as they are, I can overcome injustice, menace, terror. . . .
2. A good life is partly a matter of luck. I can look for it and cherish its intervals. But I can't control it. I can be overcome. It's going to get dark. It's going to get light. No matter my actions.

18 April 1992
When they told me bad things I always pretended to know already—for fear they would tell me more.

6 May 1992

We rabbits used to have intervals of calm and safety. We'd hop into a cozy nest in a thicket and feel good. But of late, with greatly improved means to detect danger, we feel menaced all the time. The alfalfa we eat has poisons in it. Grass may not be good for you. We constantly view rabbit oppression. We observe memorial days about rabbit roundups.

20 May 1992

All survivors are guilty.

31 May 1992

The question: How loud to cheer? Again in this valley peace has come: no one. We had a hero. The beak of history pecked away, and our great sailor is gone, riding in a tub. We indulge ourselves with monuments. If time turns around, if yesterday becomes tomorrow, who will remember today? And what would have been, beyond?

1 June 1992

Today Reality Corrupts: The spiral down.

Things get so bad that describing them is an act of obscenity. It is corrupting to deal with such reality. Those who deal with current events are damaged as human beings.

Fascination with things as they are becomes addictive; stronger and stronger shocks become necessary. People want even their entertainments to satisfy their lust for fear, cynicism, and disgust.

Staffs of periodicals, banks of moviemakers, cadres of politicians comb through garbage for their material, and thus they feed what they intend—or pretend—to decry. Their work promotes the corruption they are monitoring.

We must suspend the old course of current events in order to protect the young. And even the old, battered, disoriented, blasé can no longer register human feelings in the blizzard of our time.

Sanctuary. Sanctuary. What lives needs sanctuary.

18 October 1992
More and more my impulse is to go unnoticed. I mean, I want to be present, to take in what is happening, but not to impinge in my partial, old, unlikely way. No central position should be mine. Those around me should suffer no discomfort or troublesome reminders by my existence. Dim light, low sounds, muted presence, these should be mine.

5 November 1992
You choose your oppressor and call it government.

11 November 1992
According to instruments the whole world shudders all the time: you need to be dumb if you want to feel secure.

11 November 1992
Some people think there's a plot to infect them. That's mistaken, but even worse, they've been infected with a paranoia that makes them think there's a plot against them. The lies they tell themselves are killing them.

1 December 1992
The wider your knowledge the milder your opinions?

25 February 1993
Years happen on the farm, yes; but history happens elsewhere.

25 February 1993
In many surges of opinions and style one can see the preponderance of banality over discrimination. Bad opinions drive out good. Thoughts such as these come to mind when one reads history.

27 February 1993
The truth is, every day brings a different possibility—and a doubt about yesterday.

18 March 1993
History keeps on, though often it is sorry. We feel we might have mentioned what would have made it different. I could have changed my face, and stood longer at the parades and saluted better. Also, my tie was crooked—that discouraged my mother, who jawed my brother, who then almost lost the war, the big one.

29 June 1993
Here's how to count the people who are ready to do right: "One." "One." "One." . . .

12 July 1993
At the end of the war they let me go. Our side had won, they said. My town was gone. I didn't know I was the enemy. Attention moved, and the big eye followed me.

9 August 1993
It's a constant struggle for a human being to attain anything close to the dignity and cleanness of a rock or a piece
of wood.

15 August 1993
Don't tell me anything that requires forceful talk: that car-
ries a contradiction in its pocket. "Forceful truth" is an
oxymoron.

THREE

A Ritual to Read to Each Other

Poems

A Ritual to Read to Each Other

LEARNING

A piccolo played, then a drum.
Feet began to come—a part
of the music. Here came a horse,
clippety clop, away.

My mother said, "Don't run—
the army is after someone
other than us. If you stay
you'll learn our enemy."

Then he came, the speaker. He stood
in the square. He told us who
to hate. I watched my mother's face,
its quiet. "That's him," she said.

———

EXPLAINING THE BIG ONE

Remember that leader with the funny mustache?—
liked flags and marching?—gave loyalty
a bad name? Didn't drink, they say,
but liked music, and was jolly, sometimes.

And then the one with the big mustache
and the wrinkled uniform, always jovial
for the camera but eliminated malcontents
by the millions. He was our friend, I think.

Women? Oh yes, women. They danced
and sang for the soldiers or volunteered
their help. We loved them, except Tokyo
Rose—didn't we kill her, afterward?

Our own leaders?—the jaunty cigarette holder,
the one with the cigar. . . . Remember the pearl-handled
revolvers? And Ike, who played golf. It was us
against the bad guys, then. You should have been there.

———

AT THE BOMB TESTING SITE

At noon in the desert a panting lizard
waited for history, its elbows tense,
watching the curve of a particular road
as if something might happen.

It was looking at something farther off
than people could see, an important scene
acted in stone for little selves
at the flute end of consequences.

There was just a continent without much on it
under a sky that never cared less.
Ready for a change, the elbows waited.
The hands gripped hard on the desert.

———

AT THE GRAVE OF MY BROTHER: BOMBER PILOT

Tantalized by wind, this flag that flies
to mark your grave discourages those nearby
graves, and all still marching this hillside chanting,
    "Heroes, thanks. Good-bye."

If a visitor may quiz a marble sentiment,
was this tombstone quarried in that country
where you slew thousands likewise honored
    of the enemy?

Reluctant hero, drafted again each Fourth
of July, I'll bow and remember you. Who
shall we follow next? Who shall we kill
    next time?

———

A MESSAGE FROM
THE WANDERER

Today outside your prison I stand
and rattle my walking stick: Prisoners, listen;
you have relatives outside. And there are
thousands of ways to escape.

Years ago I bent my skill to keep my
cell locked, had chains smuggled to me in pies,
and shouted my plans to jailers;
but always new plans occurred to me,
or the new heavy locks bent hinges off,
or some stupid jailer would forget
and leave the keys.

Inside, I dreamed of constellations—
those feeding creatures outlined by stars,
their skeletons a darkness between jewels,
heroes that exist only where they are not.

Thus freedom always came nibbling my thought,
just as—often, in light, on the open hills—
you can pass an antelope and not know
and look back, and then—even before you see—
there is something wrong about the grass.
And then you see.

That's the way everything in the world is waiting.

Now—these few more words, and then I'm
gone: Tell everyone just to remember
their names, and remind others, later, when we
find each other. Tell the little ones
to cry and then go to sleep, curled up
where they can. And if any of us get lost,
if any of us cannot come all the way—
remember: there will come a time when
all we have said and all we have hoped
will be all right.

There will be that form in the grass.

———

AT THE UN-NATIONAL MONUMENT ALONG THE CANADIAN BORDER

This is the field where the battle did not happen,
where the unknown soldier did not die.
This is the field where grass joined hands,
where no monument stands,
and the only heroic thing is the sky.

Birds fly here without any sound,
unfolding their wings across the open.
No people killed—or were killed—on this ground
hallowed by neglect and an air so tame
that people celebrate it by forgetting its name.

———

PEACE WALK

We wondered what our walk should mean,
taking that un-march quietly;
the sun stared at our signs—"Thou shalt not kill."

Men by a tavern said, "Those foreigners . . ."
to a woman with a fur, who turned away—
like an elevator going down, their look at us.

Along a curb, their signs lined across,
a picket line stopped and stared
the whole width of the street, at ours: "Unfair."

Above our heads the sound truck blared—
by the park, under the autumn trees—
it said that love could fill the atmosphere:

Occur, slow the other fallout, unseen,
on islands everywhere—fallout, falling
unheard. We held our poster up to shade our eyes.

At the end we just walked away;
no one was there to tell us where to leave the signs.

WATCHING THE JET
PLANES DIVE

We must go back and find a trail on the ground
back of the forest and mountain on the slow land;
we must begin to circle on the intricate sod.
By such wild beginnings without help we may find
the small trail on through the buffalo-bean vines.

We must go back with noses and the palms of our hands,
and climb over the map in far places, everywhere,
and lie down whenever there is doubt and sleep there.
If roads are unconnected we must make a path,
no matter how far it is, or how lowly we arrive.

We must find something forgotten by everyone alive,
and make some fabulous gesture when the sun goes down
as they do by custom in little Mexico towns
where they crawl for some ritual up a rocky steep.
The jet planes dive; we must travel on our knees.

———

A RITUAL TO READ
TO EACH OTHER

If you don't know the kind of person I am
and I don't know the kind of person you are
a pattern that others made may prevail in the world
and following the wrong god home we may miss our star.

For there is many a small betrayal in the mind,
a shrug that lets the fragile sequence break
sending with shouts the horrible errors of childhood
storming out to play through the broken dyke.

And as elephants parade holding each elephant's tail,
but if one wanders the circus won't find the park,
I call it cruel and maybe the root of all cruelty
to know what occurs but not recognize the fact.

And so I appeal to a voice, to something shadowy,
a remote important region in all who talk:
though we could fool each other, we should consider—
lest the parade of our mutual life get lost in the dark.

For it is important that awake people be awake,
or a breaking line may discourage them back to sleep;
the signals we give—yes or no, or maybe—
should be clear: the darkness around us is deep.

———

THINKING FOR BERKY

In the late night listening from bed
I have joined the ambulance or the patrol
screaming toward some drama, the kind of end
that Berky must have some day, if she isn't dead.

The wildest of all, her father and mother cruel,
farming out there beyond the old stone quarry
where highschool lovers parked their lurching cars,
Berky learned to love in that dark school.

Early her face was turned away from home
toward any hardworking place; but still her soul,
with terrible things to do, was alive, looking out
for the rescue that—surely, some day—would have to come.

Windiest nights, Berky, I have thought for you,
and no matter how lucky I've been I've touched wood.
There are things not solved in our town though tomorrow
      came:
there are things time passing can never make come true.

We live in an occupied country, misunderstood;
justice will take us millions of intricate moves.
Sirens will hunt down Berky, you survivors in your beds
listening through the night, so far and good.

———

A DEDICATION

We stood by the library. It was an August night.
Priests and sisters of hundreds of unsaid creeds
passed us going their separate pondered roads.
We watched them cross under the corner light.

Freights on the edge of town were carrying away
flatcars of steel to be made into secret guns;
we knew, being human, that they were enemy guns,
and we were somehow vowed to poverty.

No one stopped or looked long or held out a hand.
They were following orders received from hour to hour,
so many signals, all strange, from a foreign power:
But tomorrow, you whispered, *peace may flow over the land.*

At that corner in a flash of lightning we two stood;
that glimpse we had will stare through the dark forever:
on the poorest roads we would be walkers and beggars,
toward some deathless meeting involving a crust of bread.

———

MEN

After a war come the memorials—
tanks, cutlasses, men with cigars.
If women are there they adore
and are saved, shielding their children.

For a long time people rehearse
just how it happened, and you have to learn
how important all that armament was—
and it really could happen again.

So the women and children can wait, whatever
their importance might have been, and they
come to stand around the memorials
and listen some more and be grateful, and smell the cigars.

Then, if your side has won, they explain
how the system works and if you just let it
go on it will prevail everywhere.
And they establish foundations and give
    some of the money back.

———

ENTERING HISTORY

Remember the line in the sand?
You were there, on the telly, part of
the military. You didn't want to
give it but they took your money
for those lethal tanks and the bombs.

Minorities, they don't have a country
even if they vote: "Thanks, anyway,"
the majority says, and you are left there
staring at the sand and the line they drew,
calling it a challenge, calling it "ours."

Where was your money when the tanks
grumbled past? Which bombs did you buy
for the death rain that fell? Which year's
taxes put that fire to the town
where the screaming began?

———

OBJECTOR

In line at lunch I cross my fork and spoon
to ward off complicity—the ordered life
our leaders have offered us. Thin as a knife,
our chance to live depends on such a sign
while others talk and The Pentagon from the moon
is bouncing exact commands: "Forget your faith;
be ready for whatever it takes to win: we face
annihilation unless all citizens get in line."

I bow and cross my fork and spoon: somewhere
other citizens more fearfully bow
in a place terrorized by their kind of oppressive state.
Our signs both mean, "You hostages over there
will never be slaughtered by my act." Our vows
cross: never to kill and call it fate.

———

SERVING WITH GIDEON

Now I remember: in our town the druggist
prescribed Coca-Cola mostly, in tapered
glasses to us, and to the elevator
man in a paper cup, so he could
drink it elsewhere because he was black.

And now I remember The Legion—gambling
in the back room, and no women but girls, old boys
who ran the town. They were generous,
to their sons or the sons of friends.
And of course I was almost one.

I remember winter light closing
its great blue fist slowly eastward
along the street, and the dark then, deep
as war, arched over a radio show
called the thirties in the great old U.S.A.

Look down, stars—I was almost
one of the boys. My mother was folding
her handkerchief; the library seethed and sparked;
right and wrong arced; and carefully
I walked with my cup toward the elevator man.

FOR THE UNKNOWN ENEMY

This monument is for the unknown
good in our enemies. Like a picture
their life began to appear: they
gathered at home in the evening
and sang. Above their fields they saw
a new sky. A holiday came
and they carried the baby to the park
for a party. Sunlight surrounded them.

Here we glimpse what our minds long turned
away from. The great mutual
blindness darkened that sunlight in the park,
and the sky that was new, and the holidays.
This monument says that one afternoon
we stood here letting a part of our minds
escape. They came back, but different.
Enemy: one day we glimpsed your life.

This monument is for you.

———

GROUND ZERO [DECEMBER 1982]

A bomb photographed me on the stone,
on a white wall, a burned outline where
the bomb rays found me out in the open
and ended me, person and shadow, never to cast
a shadow again, but be here so light

the sun doesn't know. People on Main Street
used to stand in their certain chosen places—
I walk around them. It wouldn't be right
if I stood there. But all of their shadows are mine now—
I am so white on the stone.

———

FIVE A.M.

Still dark, the early morning breathes
a soft sound above the fire. Hooded
lights on porches lead past lawns,
a hedge; I pass the house of the couple
who have the baby, the yard with the little
dog; my feet pad and grit on the pavement, flicker
past streetlights; my arms alternate
easily to my pace. Where are my troubles?

There are people in every country who never
turn into killers, saints have built
sanctuaries on islands and in valleys,
conquerors have quit and gone home, for thousands
of years farmers have worked their fields.
My feet begin the uphill curve
where a thicket spills with birds every spring.
The air doesn't stir. Rain touches my face.

———

POETRY

Its door opens near. It's a shrine
by the road, it's a flower in the parking lot
of The Pentagon, it says, "Look around,
listen. Feel the air." It interrupts
international telephone lines with a tune.
When traffic lines jam, it gets out
and dances on the bridge. If great people
get distracted by fame they forget
this essential kind of breathing
and they die inside their gold shell.
When caravans cross deserts
it is the secret treasure hidden under the jewels.

Sometimes commanders take us over, and they
try to impose their whole universe,
how to succeed by daily calculation:
I can't eat that bread.

———

SOMETHING TO DECLARE

They have never had a war big enough
to slow that pulse in the earth under
our path near that old river.

Even as a swallow swims through the air
a certain day skips and returns, hungry for
the feel and lift of the time passed by.

That was the place where I lived awhile
dragging a wing, and the spin of the world
started its tilt into where it is now.

They say that history is going on somewhere.
They say it won't stop. I have held
one picture still for a long time and waited.

This is only a little report floated
into the slow current so the wind will know
which way to come if it wants to find me.

———

ALLEGIANCES

It is time for all the heroes to go home
if they have any, time for all of us common ones
to locate ourselves by the real things
we live by.

Far to the north, or indeed in any direction,
strange mountains and creatures have always lurked—
elves, goblins, trolls, and spiders:—we
encounter them in dread and wonder,

But once we have tasted far streams, touched the gold,
found some limit beyond the waterfall,
a season changes, and we come back, changed
but safe, quiet, grateful.

Suppose an insane wind holds all the hills
while strange beliefs whine at the traveler's ears,
we ordinary beings can cling to the earth and love
where we are, sturdy for common things.

———

OUR KIND

Our mother knew our worth—
not much. To her, success
was not being noticed at all.
"If we can stay out of jail,"
she said, "God will be proud of us."

"Not worth a row of pins,"
she said, when we looked at the album:
"Grandpa?—ridiculous."
Her hearing was bad, and that
was good: "None of us ever says much."

She sent us forth equipped
for our kind of world, a world of
our betters, in a nation so strong
its greatest claim is no boast,
its leaders telling us all, "Be proud"—

But over their shoulders, God and
our mother, signaling: "Ridiculous."

———

HOW IT IS

It is war. They put us on a train and
say, "Go." A bell wakes up the engine
as we move along past the crowd,
and a child—one clear small gaze from all the town—
finds my face. I wave. For long I look
back. "I'm not a soldier," I want to say.
But the gaze is left behind. And I'm gone.

———

1 9 4 0

It is August. Your father is walking you
to the train for camp and then the War
and on out of his life, but you don't know.

Little lights along the path glow under their hoods
and your shoes go brown, brown in the brightness
till the next interval, when they disappear in the shadow.

You know they are down there, by the crunch of stone
and a rustle when they touch a fern. Somewhere above,
cicadas arch their gauze of sound all over town.

Shivers of summer wind follow across the park
and then turn back. You walk on toward
September, the depot, the dark, the light, the dark.

———

IN CAMP

That winter of the war, every day
sprang outward. I was a prisoner.
Someone brought me gifts. That year
now is far: birds can't fly
the miles to find a forgotten cause.

No task I do today has justice
at the end. All I know is
my degree of leaning in this wind
where—once the mind springs free—
every cause has reason
but reason has no law.

In camps like that, if I should go again,
I'd still study the gospel and play the accordion.

———

GROUND ZERO [JUNE 1982]

While we slept—
        rain found us last night, easing in
        from the coast, a few leaves at first,
        then ponds. The quietest person in the state
        heard the mild invasion. Before it was over
        every field knew that benediction.

At breakfast—
    while we talked some birds passed, then slanted
    north, wings emphasizing earth's weight
    but overcoming it. "There's no hope,"
    you said. Our table had some flowers
    cascading color from their vase. Newspapers
    muttered repression and shouted revolution.
    A breeze lifted curtains; they waved
    easily. "Why can't someone do something!"
    My hand began its roving, like those curtains,
    and the flowers bending, and the far-off bird wings.

———

THE ANIMAL THAT DRANK UP SOUND

I

One day across the lake where echoes come now
an animal that needed sound came down. He gazed
enormously, and instead of making any, he took
away from, sound: the lake and all the land
went dumb. A fish that jumped went back like a knife,
and the water died. In all the wilderness around he
drained the rustle from the leaves into the mountainside
and folded a quilt over the rocks, getting ready
to store everything the place had known; he buried—
thousands of autumns deep—the noise that used to come there.

Then that animal wandered on and began to drink
the sound out of all the valleys—the croak of toads,
and all the little shiny noise grass blades make.
He drank till winter, and then looked out one night
at the stilled places guaranteed around by frozen
peaks and held in the shallow pools of starlight.
It was finally tall and still, and he stopped on the highest
ridge, just where the cold sky fell away
like a perpetual curve, and from there he walked on silently,
and began to starve.

When the moon drifted over the night the whole world lay
just like the moon, shining back that still
silver, and the moon saw its own animal dead
on the snow, its dark absorbent paws and quiet
muzzle, and thick, velvet, deep fur.

2

After the animal that drank sound died, the world
lay still and cold for months, and the moon yearned
and explored, letting its dead light float down
the west walls of canyons and then climb its delighted
soundless way up the east side. The moon
owned the earth its animal had faithfully explored.
The sun disregarded the life it used to warm.

But on the north side of a mountain, deep in some rocks,
a cricket slept. It had been hiding when that animal
passed, and as spring came again this cricket waited,
afraid to crawl out into the heavy stillness.

Think how deep the cricket felt, lost there
in such a silence—the grass, the leaves, the water,
the stilled animals all depending on such a little
thing. But softly it tried—"Cricket!"—and back like a river
from that one act flowed the kind of world we know,
first whisperings, then moves in the grass and leaves;
the water splashed, and a big night bird screamed.

It all returned, our precious world with its life and sound,
where sometimes loud over the hill the moon,
wild again, looks for its animal to roam, still,
down out of the hills, any time.
But somewhere a cricket waits.

It listens now, and practices at night.

———

THE STAR IN THE HILLS

A star hit in the hills behind our house
up where the grass turns brown touching the sky.

Meteors have hit the world before, but this was near,
and since TV; few saw, but many felt the shock.
The state of California owns that land
(and out from shore three miles), and any stars
that come will be roped off and viewed on week days 8 to 5.

A guard who took the oath of loyalty and denied
any police record told me this:
"If you don't have a police record yet
you could take the oath and get a job
if California should be hit by another star."

"I'd promise to be loyal to California
and to guard any stars that hit it," I said,
"or any place three miles out from shore,
unless the star was bigger than the state—
in which case, I'd be loyal to *it.*"

But he said no exceptions were allowed,
and he leaned against the state-owned meteor
so calm and puffed a cork-tip cigarette
that I looked down and traced with my foot in the dust
and thought again and said, "OK—any star."

———

CLASH

The butcher knife was there
on the table my father made.
The hatchet was on the stair;
I knew where it was.

Hot wires burned in the wall,
all the nails pointed in.
At the sound of my mother's call
I knew it was the time.

When she threatened I hid in the yard.
Policemen would come for me.
It was dark; waiting was hard.
There was something I had to win.

After my mother wept
I forgot where the hatchet was:
there was a truce we kept—
we both chose real things.

If she taunted, I grew still.
If she faltered, I lowered the knife.
I did not have to kill.
Time had made me stronger.

I won before too late,
and—adult before she died—
I had traveled from love to hate,
and partway back again.

Now all I have, my life,
—strange—comes partly from this:
I thought about a knife
when I learned that great word—"Choose."

———

6 August, Hiroshima Day
NOVEMBER

From the sky in the form of snow
comes the great forgiveness.
Rain grown soft, the flakes descend
and rest; they nestle close, each one
arrived, welcomed and then at home.

If the sky lets go some day and I'm
requested for such volunteering
toward so clean a message, I'll come.
The world goes on and while friends touch down
beside me, I too will come.

———

28 August 1993
"ARE YOU MR. WILLIAM STAFFORD?"

"Are you Mr. William Stafford?"
"Yes, but. . . ."

Well, it was yesterday.
Sunlight used to follow my hand.
And that's when the strange siren-like sound flooded
over the horizon and rushed through the streets of our town.
That's when sunlight came from behind
a rock and began to follow my hand.

"It's for the best," my mother said—"Nothing can
ever be wrong for anyone truly good."
So later the sun settled back and the sound
faded and was gone. All along the streets every
house waited, white, blue, gray; trees
were still trying to arch as far as they could.

You can't tell when strange things with meaning
will happen. I'm [still] here writing it down
just the way it was. "You don't have to
prove anything," my mother said. "Just be ready
for what God sends." I listened and put my hand
out in the sun again. It was all easy.

Well, it was yesterday. And the sun came,
Why
It came.

FAMILY STATEMENT

My brother, flying a plane in this war,
    may come up that long ramp to the exit
    and go into tomorrow.
He may turn his face away from our small play by the
    mulberry tree, and kill a man.
(And every day I put my hand on the stone wall at the corner,
    turning and looking back;
I wear the old hat, and the tie he sent.)

My brother is in the army that wins, swearing, proud of a flag.
The movie stars are making him happy,
    taking those long trips we read about and see pictures of.
The common soldier is hero in this war:
        my brother was one hundred yards away in the crowd
        when a private, in a ceremony on a stage, kissed Tana Randis
        (currently seen in "Land of Desire").
(And every morning my feet hurry the leaves under these trees.
I won't walk another street until this one is worn out by the sun.)

My brother, in the army that wins, and I
    remember those many times when Pop came home from trips
    and everyone meeting him at the door.
My brother and I are both crying
    in this glittering chromium time
    in the saddest war.

———

DECEMBER

Take a late, blue, winter evening. If you
wait till it's dark enough, and you go
stand in the cold where town ends, and look
for last light in the west—that's my last
year at college, waiting to be drafted
and wondering how the world would end.

———

CHILDREN STILL PLAY

Children still play, but their elders, who know, are afraid:
a silent, peaceful army has occupied the land
with stealthy, unseen sharpshooters, fragments of strontium,
so casual and lethal an enemy it salutes everyone,
inside a fort and out. Touched by those waves,
the great are joined in so tiny a dance they think
their world still: their yachts ride the deep, their mansions
gaze over lakes, a conspiracy nobody feels.

Generals bend over their plans, and this is the way
it is done: "We move, they move, and we all embrace
that little, fine rain that comes." An end like that
has always been in the plans—death will always
provide company for the dead—
when Moses was on the mountain that is what God said.

———

MACHO HISTORY

Xerxes, and whoever it was raging
on the other side, they had some foot-dragging,
just-as-soon-skip-it followers,
you can bet. And some of those heroic
women didn't die but fraternized
with the enemy and began to like them, maybe.

Over in Athens when the slaves cheered
for their conquerors, that's when you knew
some past war was, thank God, finally
forgotten. "A national hero is a national
disaster," some German said, who
ought to know, standing there looking around.

But conquerors don't usually learn very fast,
only thinkers and poets sometimes—Buddha, Teresa, Jesus.

———

A MEMORIAL

In Nagasaki they have built a little room
dark and soundproof where you can
go in all alone and close the door and cry.

———

PRETEND YOU LIVE IN A ROOM

Play like you had a war. Hardly anyone
got killed except thousands of the enemy,
and many go around starving, holding
their hands out in pictures, begging.

Their houses, even the concrete and iron,
they've disappeared. These people
now live camped in the open. Overhead
stars keep telling their old, old story.

You have this world. You wander the earth.
You can't live in a room.

———

STATE OF THE UNION

While we all were brave, listening to The President
speak, my cousin coughed out a story, how
every soldier, each with a rifle and a shadow,
stepped forward to receive a decoration. How
then they counted the shadows and one was missing—
found later wandering from war to war, confused
among the dead on either side, trying
to give away that ribbon all covered with blood.

My cousin coughed out that story
at the last, holding out the proof in her hand,
but unable to remember if it was given
by their side or our side, or by that spook,
a refugee lost from every army.

———

THEY SUFFER FOR US

In war so many come
you hardly notice one,
but a little child killed by a bomb
and borne away,
that image lasts for a while.

These times have taken our world
and turned it into a play,
your soldiers cursing, and ours,
and certain great people
being brave and principled and sure.

They are different from us, the great
I mean. It is hard to be right
all the time, as they have to be
no matter what happens. And we,
to repay their suffering for us—

We cheer when we die for their tears.

———

LOSERS

Along the coast and all along those interior rivers
that bind places too quiet for missiles or treaties
we are the victims, the hostages, of the Twentieth Century.

Others have won it all, the national brands, the rubbing
and whisper of civilization's intricate software.

Their children feed money into machines and then swoon
through the plot of The Great Moloch Fairytale: winning.

We can feel the slide into maximum g's of acceleration;
we can feel it as we walk their parks, their controlled wilderness
or the paradigm plazas with banners and music and ads.

Well, we can be losers here and stand it while the weather is warm
and soothing, and the others keep cheering and hugging each other
and waving little flags.

———

FOR THE OREGON HOUSE
SESSION, 13 APRIL 1987

This hall recalls that one where warriors watched
a sparrow fly from darkness, traverse their banquet
table, and disappear into the night:
that flight symbolized a life, and the warriors
heard, in Anselm's story, how every person appears
from the unknown, enjoys light, and goes alone
away from this world into the dark.

A like sojourn is ours today:
out in the woods and salal, in the rabbitbrush
and sage, along the coast, up in the mountains,
Oregon waits. Days and nights will pass:
our people will watch and wonder. Secure here,
we can stumble and still govern, trusted: but always
parts of our state will depend on this hall.

Only the people voted, but the animals too are there,
and the salmon testing silt in their home rivers.
Even the trees deserve a place, and the hills
maintaining their part, while the rocks are quietly
mentioning integrity.

We start. We cherish this hall, and keep it
for justice and all good works, and for the world we have
while we traverse its warmth and light,
inheritors from those who went before
and keepers of faith for those who are to come.

———

FOUR

Some Questions about Victory

Notes, Statements, and Interviews on Pacifism

Some Questions about Victory

I AM A PACIFIST

1. Valuing noninterference, but speaking when asked.

2. Commitment useful when speaking briefly.

3. Some useful parallels:

   a) What would I do if our country were invaded some morning without provocation? (What would you do if our country invaded another some morning without provocation?)

   b) What would I do if someone attacked my grandmother? (What would you do if one of your family attacked someone?)

   c) What would I do if someone attacked me, some vicious wild man? (What would you do if someone equated the established policy of your country—with its public debate, its various processes—with those of a wild man?)

These parallels all lend themselves to quick solving: they reveal that arguments used against pacifism are short circuits of more realistic judgments: we must turn to more serious levels.

4. Some worthy questions:

a) Do you think any reduction in the "war making" of "enemy" powers can be induced in any way except by force? (Corollary: Could they reduce our war making against them by any means other than power? Additional corollary: How do you account for or justify using one means of reasoning when predicting your own behavior, and another means when predicting theirs?)

b) Of any influence you could use on other nations— whether power or otherwise—which persons in that other nation would it bear on? All alike? Some more than others? Is there any value in influencing other persons, even those not in power abroad? (Corollary: If there is no value in such influence of noncrucial persons abroad, what value is there in your influencing me? Further corollary: If you don't care about me, is it all right if I persuade great numbers of others to my position?)

c) Thinking about our own country, are there ways to use our power abroad which will weaken our own commitment to our national policy? Then would it be wise to use our power with care, so as to carry along public opinion? And does public opinion, in fact, depend partly on the human impulses of you and me and others? Then opinion *does* make a difference? Is it then realistic to consider it? And even pacifist feelings count?

5. A problem for anyone engaging without question in his country's foreign policy, including war:

a) If you take the oath required of a soldier, are you permitted to hold reservations about some kinds of acts you will not do?

b) Have soldiers in our military forces been required by their superiors to engage in acts you would refuse to do? Can you envision any such? Where would you draw the line? Would you release the atom bomb over any city? Would you fly the plane? Would you fuel it? Would you order it to fly? Would you transmit such orders? Would you train its bombardier? Would you manufacture a bomb useful only for saturation attack? Would you hold religious services in order to sustain the morale of people engaged in such acts?

c) Would you fly missions like the ones to bomb Dresden? (Repeat of questions above.)

d) Do you consider the acts of some foreign troops criminal? Do you believe in war crimes? Does the identification of a "war crime" in fact obligate us to recognize that there are deeds not to be done under any provocation, or as part of any policy?

6. Is there any place in life today for persons who announce beforehand that they will not engage in carrying out the tasks implied in the current policies of military men? Would you like to see such people exist abroad? In China? In Germany? In Russia?

They do exist. Some were killed. Does their sacrifice
release me from serving the vision we saw?
Should I bomb their relatives and
friends? My allegiance
is to our
vision.

I am a pacifist.

*An unpublished statement typed by Stafford in the 1960s. To use
parallel questions (one applying to this country, and the other
sending the mind forth to consider another country) was his
habit when discussing military issues.*

———

LAKE GROVE PRESBYTERIAN
CONFERENCE ON VIETNAM,
5 OCTOBER 1966

"It is in the minds of men that peace is won."

1. To contest in a debate and lose your own soul. . . . We
   meet for a very brief interval; our decisions are made with
   our lives. Later, think of this place, the timing of points
   made, the sequence of speakers. Use the occasion, but do
   not *rely* on it.

2. If the next move were our own personal commitment,
   in a landing boat, flying a bomber, negotiating, deciding
   whether we could save or not save a person—would we decide as we do when discussing? Would we try harder for

alternatives? Do we fully realize what we commit people to when we decide on a war?

We are not debating whether China is likely to enter, etc., or the successful use of force. But *should* we so force the world?

3. The crucial issues before us are almost by definition not clear: we have conflicting authorities. Tonight we are not going to have anyone present who knows more in favor of pursuing the war than the president, or his secretary of state, or any officer involved. We are not going to have a critic better informed than Fulbright, or de Gaulle, or Ho Chi Minh, or the pope, or U Thant. We have been flooded with information, but we must decide for ourselves.

4. In our own country we live inside a wall of sound; our own positions get elaborate production. If we make a peace move that is turned down, we know it. How many peace moves by individual people on the "opposing" side have been made? Have any been turned down? How many infiltrators from South Vietnam are in North Vietnam? Are all members of Ho Chi Minh's family equally bloodthirsty? Is there a Fulbright, even an incipient, timid Fulbright, in China? One must go abroad to get the great, sudden drench of noninvolved opinion. That opinion has crescendoed against U.S. actions recently.

5. The strongest nation in the world, with no present danger to itself, acting without formal declaration of war, under firm military conscription, has burned, used gas, threatened atomic force, systematically invaded noninvolved nations. Restraint must come from citizens. Hence our

meeting. Coercion by violence has hardened much of the world; that feeling lasts. But moderating it is the patient, worthy job.

6. We dominate the world; for the future it is essential that we reach community, not supremacy. The danger currently is to others. Can we guarantee the conduct of our state? Would Nixon use restraint? Would Goldwater? Would Kennedy? Do we so purely operate that we can decide to use any necessary means to win?

7. Politicians need citizens who will permit them to behave reasonably. We must see in time that public opinion does enable rational leaders to moderate conflict. We can lose; we can pull back; we can seek not domination but conciliation.

Stafford's notes for his part in a discussion at the Lake Grove Presbyterian Church, near his home in Lake Oswego, Oregon.

———

ON WAR AND PEACE

INTERVIEWER: *World War II has always been presented as a necessary war—there was a threat. Yet to come upon people who had the presence of mind in those times to be conscientious objectors always seems overwhelming to me.*

STAFFORD: You would have found company back then, too. When I was in high school, probably in grade school, this sort of thing gets going when you have a war, this kind of juggernaut that goes and, whether it's just or not when it starts, turns into something else. You begin to pick that up among "intellectuals," is it possible to say? So all through the thirties, my teachers in the social sciences, and others too, were aware of what was coming, and kept saying it was coming. . . . Then something like Pearl Harbor happens and they say we're having the war because of Pearl Harbor. It's an incident, but it was going to happen.

What was the reaction to you and fellow COs? I imagine it to be much harsher in World War II than it was in the Vietnam era.

It was a lot harsher. I can remember one of my close college friends saying, "You just ought to be machine-gunned." And he lived down the hall; he was my friend. So I said, "You don't mean that. You couldn't really machine-gun me." He said, "Maybe not, but I could drop a bomb." He was a radical, by the way, and vociferous against the war before it happened. But he got caught right up in it.

That's what I envision the reaction to have been. People might have said, "No, no, no, let's not do this," up until it happened. Then they all went for it.

Almost everyone around me did, including my family. My brother went into the air force and my sister's husband was in the navy. That was how it was all up and down the block. Only a very few quiet, quiet people came around and said, "How you doing, Bill?" They weren't walking down the street saying, "Good, good."

How was it within your family?

The family was very close; it was harmonious. My mother had been antiwar all my life. She wouldn't let me join the Boy Scouts because they were too warlike. Later I found out she was right. At the time, though, I thought she was really quaint. But I didn't join the Boy Scouts, because they wore uniforms like those Nazis. . . .

When the war was over, was it held against you?

I think most people wanted to forget it. Some didn't want to, and probably a few people still don't forget it. But I'm familiar with this feeling—you come out of all the turmoil and you had a certain role. Now what's your role? "What did you do in the war, Daddy?" . . .

. . . There were jobs, though, that I couldn't take because of my beliefs. For instance, at that time, many state universities required military training, ROTC. I was offered jobs at such places, but I'd have to tell them I couldn't teach at a place where the students have to do something I think is wrong. . . .

During the sixties, every now and then, someone would meet me and say, "We're opposing the Vietnam War and I heard that you were a CO way back when." I never thought that it would be an honor. We all thought that for the rest of our lives we would be hiding. . . .

I've been curious about the fact that the COs at Waldport were printing things during the war. While it wasn't obviously political, that was something, being in the position they were in.

It was different than the Vietnam War, which wasn't a war technically or legally, so you could do all sorts of things. In World War II, there were a lot of things you couldn't do, and there were immediate, move-in-and-suppress type actions. I never experienced any myself, but it went on. The camps put out all sorts of stuff, and they weren't at all reverent or careful.

I'm a good citizen myself and I never did meet anybody I thought was subversive. The camp was a good place to find subversives, but I never found a one. There was reckless talk, and they did exercise free speech, and some of the people were quite caustic about some congressmen and the president.

Why, I still remember a wonderful scene where a fellow in camp in Arkansas lined us up and said, "Now men, it has come to my attention that some of you men been callin' Nigra men 'Mister' and Nigra women 'Missus.' This has got to stop." Well you knew no one there was going to obey him. They all sort of shuffled their feet and let him finish his speech. He knew they weren't going to follow what he said.

From "William Stafford on War and Peace," an interview by Stephen Sander, published in Spectrum *2, no. 1 (Spring 1978).*

———

THAT ANSWER'S NOT GOOD ENOUGH

STAFFORD: I've had trouble with people in political discussions about pacifism, and so on. I remember once taking a stand: Well, I can't stop war. Jesus couldn't stop war. Eisenhower couldn't stop war. Why should I blame myself for not stopping war? What I can do is to do the things that are within my power. I can decide there's one person who won't be in it. That's a possibility. But I can't stop it, and someone who was there kept saying, "Well, that answer's not good enough for me." You know, he had this John Wayne reaction: "I'm going to stop it." That leads you to terrorist acts that don't really do any good, but they relieve your conscience. I don't want to relieve my conscience; I want to do good.

From "An Interview with William Stafford," a transcript of an unpublished interview by Steven Hind, conducted in Hutchinson, Kansas, on February 6, 1983. A version of Hind's interview was published in Cottonwood, *no. 34 (Fall 1984).*

BE PROUD

INTERVIEWER: *Your poems about America seem to be almost despairing. There's the fear of not having any privacy. And then there's the poem about the media buying everybody's life. Do you feel that way about America? Do you have a fear for it?*

STAFFORD: Yes I do. It's there; many Americans feel this. It was different if you grew up during a time when the United States was not . . . spying, CIA, grabbing the world and making it go the way they wanted it to go. When America had bravado because it didn't have power. And now it's got too much, you know, that's the feeling. I even have this poem where I say, "Its greatest claim is no boast, / its leaders telling us all, 'Be proud'—" There's a nervousness about taking such a stance, the feeling that many of my friends have that we're caught up on an ongoing juggernaut. I couldn't find anyone who had voted for Reagan, among our friends, and then there's this feeling, knowing a lot of people out there voted for him. Realizing that your nation is no longer your home.

I don't feel anti-American; I feel the same way about a lot of the low-down things being done all over the world. It's just that maybe that note comes into the writings of some Americans now. You get a glimpse of political situations we used to think we were responsible for, and we're no longer at the steering wheel. Emerson said, "Things are in the saddle, and ride mankind." He felt it way back then. It took me a long time to see that, but it shows up in some of the poems.

From "William Stafford," an interview by Kevin Connolly, published in What!, *nos. 28 and 29 (December 1991).*

———

OUT IN THE COLD

INTERVIEWER: *How do you feel that your years during World War II affected your writing?*

STAFFORD: Those years in camp, isolated, four years, isolated from the rest of society, for a long time I thought they didn't really make any difference. I mean it's just as if you're gone and then you're back. And that's just something that happened. It didn't really influence your life. More recently

I felt that was an abiding influence. Not in any spectacular way, not in any way that would show up in the society around me. For instance I did get a job. And I wasn't really troubled except in slant ways, for a very brief time after World War II, by the CO position. So outwardly it wasn't very apparent. But I've come to feel that probably inwardly I was very much influenced by those four years. The habit of getting up early and writing every day, the sort of—strange to say this—fortress mentality and of being a part of a little group that's apart from society. The automatic assumption that one didn't have to conform; in fact conformity was a danger sign. I fought against that. I wanted to be a part of society, but I think the steady realization that one could be different and apart, on a day-by-day basis without questioning oneself about it, couldn't help having an influence on the writing habits and on the habits of mind that made you different from and ready to be different from the society around you. That must have had an influence on my writing. And more recently I've thought, maybe because I feel it less extremely now than I did then, that all those years part of my writing was fueled by the need to hold out against pressure from outside, society's pressure, government's pressure, or the pressure of people around me.

It became a habit of mind that encouraged me or strengthened me to be more rigorously independent of any kind of pressure from people—even people near me. You don't unlearn in a hurry those readinesses to take a stand, even a stand that may not be trumpeted but is very seriously held on all kinds of issues, any kind of issue. A kind of side-slipping of the social pressure that would hit other people but doesn't hit you. Even from your friends, even from your family, and a kind of a coldness, I think, is in my writing, and maybe in myself, as a result of being out in the cold for four crucial years.

From the transcript of an unpublished interview by Vince Wixon and Mike Markee, conducted in Newport, Oregon, in November 1987. A portion of this interview was included in William Stafford: What the River Says, *videocassette, directed by Wixon and Markee, TTTD Productions, 1989.*

———

THE OTHER PEOPLE CHANGED

INTERVIEWER: *Even though you liked the place you grew up, you left home eventually.*

STAFFORD: Oh well, I went to other places because I was forced to: I was drafted; they made me go. It took World War II to get me out of Kansas. I was going to the University of Kansas graduate school and the draft board said, "Go." First Arkansas, then California, then Illinois, and it ended by my traveling a lot, yes. I'm an illustration of Newton's laws: the object at rest tends to stay at rest, unless compelled by some energy to go elsewhere.

Why did you become a conscientious objector?

Strangely, I didn't become one; I always was one. I thought all right-thinking people would behave that way. In those days, the 1930s, the peace movement was strong in America.

In fact, Franklin Roosevelt, to get elected, had to promise "no war." The other people changed, and I was surprised. I thought a commitment was a commitment. There were peace people everywhere, in all countries, and I was not about to break ranks with that worldwide fellowship.

From "The Art of Poetry LXVII," an interview by William Young, published in Paris Review *35, no. 129 (1993).*

———

THE LONG HAUL

Keep a journal, and don't assume that your work has to accomplish anything worthy: artists and peace-workers are in it for the long haul, and not to be judged by immediate results. . . .

. . . Redemption comes with care. In our culture we can oppose but not subvert. Openness is part of our technique.

From "Making Peace Among the Words," a lecture given at Bluffton College, Bluffton, Ohio, March 20, 1990.

———

IT'S A MADNESS ALMOST EVERYONE HAS

It's a madness almost everyone has, war
years, to choose a person to hate
and get hated by. It's hard to get back

where the world was when the war's over,
but almost everyone does. A few, though,
keep on, getting ready for next time.
That hate makes the war necessary.

*From an unpublished poem written March 4, 1991, under the
spell of the Gulf War.*

———

A POLICE FORCE IS NOT AN ARMY

A police action should be fair, consistent, directed toward
the criminals alone, subject to review, carried out by dis-
interested parties, commensurate with the crime. . . .

The establishing of security by terror is to create enemies
and counterterror. Security through goodwill is universally
recognized (creating friends, alliances, mutual dependence),
even by dictators.

*From an unpublished note written March 11, 1991. In discus-
sions, Stafford would frequently use the analogy of a police force
(created by citizens for common cause) as a counter example to
the work of a national army (created by citizens of one country
for attack on another).*

———

SOME QUESTIONS
ABOUT VICTORY

Is there a quiet way, a helpful way, to question what has been won in a war that the victors are still cheering? Can questions be asked without slighting that need to celebrate the relief of a war quickly ended?

Or does the winning itself close out questions about it? Might failing to question it make it easier to try a war again?

Maybe a successful performance that kills tens of thousands, that results in the greatest pollution in history, that devastates a nation, that helps confirm governments in their reliance on weapons for security—maybe such an action deserves a cautious assessment? Maybe some people might be forgiven a few thoughtful moments amid the cheering?

Does it increase feelings of security to find that your leader can commit country and Congress to a line in the sand and then challenge world opinion to make a choice between that individual commitment and the appearance of being weak?

Does an outcome that surprised everyone confirm your faith in overwhelming armament as the mode of security for your country?

If so, do you think that other countries may reach a similar conclusion? Has establishing the superiority of your own terror made you feel secure against the terror that others have learned to be so effective?

If someone blindfolded leads others across the busy freeway and finds with surprise only slight injuries, would that

success justify faith in a guide like that? Does survival prove
the guide's wisdom?

How can dominance be accepted in a world community
based on fairness? Was the recent war helpful in moving in
that direction?

Can we bear to see our peace dividend go glimmering in
the aftermath of a war that made overwhelming armament
seem so dazzling? Is there a way to maintain hope for policies
that will enable security and justice without the necessity of
battle or the threat of battle led by America?

Is peace in fact served well if intoxicating victory is cele-
brated by the strongest nation in the world.

Listen to me; listen slow:

In—this—war—again—humanity—lost.

A statement published in Hungry Mind Review, *no. 18*
(Summer 1991).

———

A PRIEST OF THE IMAGINATION

INTERVIEWER: *What were you doing immediately before*
[World War II]?

STAFFORD: When I was drafted, in 1942, just a week or so
after Pearl Harbor, I was well into my program toward a
master's degree in English at the University of Kansas, and
after my four years of captivity in the camps I went back and
picked up the degree, with the help of my manuscript written

during the time in camp. That manuscript became my first book, *Down in My Heart,* published by the Church of the Brethren, for whom I had served. The book was an account of those four years in camp.

You have said that on your way to the camp you had a copy of John Woolman's Journal *with you.*

Right. My teacher gave me that as I was leaving. I don't think she talked directly to me about my being a conscientious objector. This was the time when people were scattering for military camps in all directions from the University of Kansas. But I thought about it later. I think she didn't say anything to me because there was no need to say anything. She was a Quaker and gave me *The Journal of John Woolman,* and when I read it, I saw.

. . . Were you writing poetry during those years?

As an undergraduate I had majored in both English and economics, for I wanted to write but also wanted to help overcome the damage of the depression. My reading all slid toward literature, though, and I turned from the field of economics. My time in camp had confirmed in me the habit of daily writing, and in all the years since I have continued the habit. The result has been a torrent of manuscripts, many of them lurking in my attic. . . .

You have been active in the Fellowship of Reconciliation. What exactly has been your role in that and similar organizations?

Being a war resister, deliberately taking on the role of being different, permeated my life with an outside attitude. In college I had engaged in sit-ins opposing segregation in the University of Kansas Union Building, which, like many other places, refused service to blacks. This was along in the late 1930s. We always felt that our stand then helped lead toward the later protests that caught the world's attention. In World War II some of us couldn't help feeling the irony of sending troops across the world to fight injustice when a black person would be denied fair treatment at home. So, I joined the War Resisters League and the Fellowship of Reconciliation. My wife and I have our fifty-year certificate from the FOR, and our friends are largely associated with such organizations and movements. We have always assumed that such stands as we take may cost us, and in extreme instances, as in World War II for me, the cost may be significant. But generally we find ourselves and our views welcomed: I cherish the esteem of those around me, and voice my protest in such a way as to reconcile rather than to offend. . . .

Is there any connection between your attitude toward quiet and silence and your own method of writing? . . .

. . . I feel congenial to what you just said, partly because for me the experience of finding the way in writing is one of sensitivity, listening, glimpsing, going forward by means of little signals, and those little signals are available in conditions of quiet, lack of turbulence, and conditions that are nonconfrontational. Thinking, forensic thinking, is a nonsense term to me. I think that one finds one's way with a sensibility that requires an attitude other than loudness or aggression. . . .

*. . . You have such faith in people and that anyone can write. . . .
The faith that somehow there is that within everyone which can
manifest itself in writing and in an authentic way seems to be
very comfortable for you.*

It is comfortable for me, I think, for a number of reasons.
For instance, Kierkegaard had this: everybody's equal, not in
the Jeffersonian sense, but equal in the face of the magnitude
of what we don't know. Human presumption about the more
or less is quaint; you know, it's provincial, it's a provinciality
to make much of that.

I wrote an article called "A Priest of the Imagination" to
give at a gathering of English teachers, and in it there is this
faith, this idea: I'm a priest of the imagination, and when
I go to class my job is conducting the inner light of those
people to wherever it's going. . . .

*In what way might you see your poetry as being related to your
lifelong commitment to peace?*

I suppose that the life of writing does conduce to sustained
thinking and the consideration of consequences beyond
the immediate and superficial. It is sort of like that question about why I worked. I thought every respectable person
did. I still feel that way, and look for goodwill and humanity
everywhere, including among "the enemy."

*From "A Priest of the Imagination," an interview by David
Elliott, published in* Friends Journal *(November 1991).*

———

A GESTURE TOWARD AN
UNFOUND RENAISSANCE

Your straying feet find the great dance,
walking alone.
And you live on a world where stumbling
always leads home.

Year after year fits over your face—
when there was youth, your talent
was youth;
later, you find your way by touch
where moss redeems the stone;

And you discover where music begins
before it makes any sound,
far in the mountains where canyons go
still as the always-falling, ever-new flakes of snow.

This purposeful wandering that we represent, the arts, this
turning away from the rigorously planned and effective pro-
cedure that has made us be in control of things—today this
essential play feels more important than ever.

By shunning our feelings, by postponing the results of
our actions till research is completed, and then by applying
stern technique to machines or weapons—this science and
technology life has wrapped us in ease and security. But
our human feelings are deprived. We hardly dare consider
at length what manner of life we have accepted in order
to maintain our control over *things*. The weapons poised

over our heads and the industry that supplies our needs—
these have a cost that our escape into art helps us to live
with. And we do possess means to carry us into salvation,
at intervals.

ATWATER KENT (LATE NIGHT RADIO)

Late nights the world flooded our dark house
in a dim throbbing from a glowing little box, velvety
sound hovering from horns, or Cab Calloway
far in a night club that stretched all the way to Kansas.

Maybe rewarded with popcorn or fudge, maybe
just exhausted by the day, we sprawled on the living room
rug and were carried above our house, out
over town, and spread thin by a violin.

Once from Chicago Ennio Bolognini
civilized with his cello a whole
hemisphere, and we were transformed into Italians
or other great people, listening in palaces.

Rich in our darkness, we lay inheriting
rivers of swirling millions, and the promise of never
a war again. It all came from the sky,
Heaven: London, Rome, Copenhagen.

Borrowing the title of this piece from one of his published poems,
"A Gesture Toward an Unfound Renaissance," and beginning

this writing with three stanzas from another of his poems, "You and Art," Stafford weaves poetry and memory into an unpublished personal statement. As with many of his recollections from childhood in Kansas, he imagines our future by seeking to recover the lost good thing.

GANDHI QUESTIONS, CITIZEN QUESTIONS, TRENDS OF THOUGHT

Can a good person be a good citizen in a bad country? Is
    there such a thing?
Can a good person be a good friend of a bad person?
Can you speak truth to power?
How loud do you have to say no to an evil command?
Can you safely say yes?
They give you a flag and watch to see how hard you
    wave it.
Should your effort be to overcome those who oppose the good
    as you see it?—or should you try to redeem them? No mat-
    ter who . . .

SEVEN SINS DEFINED BY GANDHI

Wealth without work.
Pleasure without conscience.
Knowledge without character.
Commerce without morality.

Science without humanity.
Worship without sacrifice.
Politics without principle.

Stafford's notes for a high-school class discussion of pacifism. If invited, he would volunteer to visit classes to discuss writing, the creative process, and a life of witness.

———

SHOW ME A GOOD WAR

INTERVIEWER: *As a committed pacifist who did not serve militarily in the Second World War, what are your thoughts on the recent war in the Gulf?*

STAFFORD: I was appalled by this war. Like many others. I thought they did the wrong thing. I mean, incinerating all those people. Riling up the whole world. A colossal failure of understanding, of the possibilities. Failure of imagination. A swashbuckling excursion that may have consequences. Creating stable conditions takes deftness, the accumulation of world opinions. It's better if you can begin to make it happen by millions of intricate little adjustments. But every now and then someone sees a short trip, thinks, "Well, we can neglect the secondary effects of this, and we can decisively win this war, so let's do it." And as a human being, a hostage to those things happening above us, you know, let's see if we can do it without killing so many people.

So you are opposed to war. Period.

I am. I remember the person beside me in a cot in Arkansas [at the CO camp in 1942]. He just got his Ph.D. in philosophy from Harvard. His draft board called him in:

"Oh, so you're opposed to war. All wars? Even a good war?"

He said, "Show me a good one."

From "William Stafford: An Interview by Thomas E. Kennedy," published in American Poetry Review 22, no. 3 (May/June 1993).

———

SPEAK TRUTH TO POWER

STAFFORD: [There's] a little interior rhetoric in our family: to see and to assess and really not to oppose, but not to go along either. I mean a kind of a Quaker point of view: "Speak truth to power." Do you know that phrasing from the Quakers?

INTERVIEWER: *No . . .*

"Speak truth to power." And so neither lie down and roll over, nor be aggressive.

I had never read Down in My Heart *before this spring. I loved that book.*

Well, being a pacifist in a nation at war, in World War II, a very popular war, was four years of reinforcement of my mother's point of view. It was graduate work in my mother's attitude. . . . Human beings are not awesome. Human beings are vulnerable. And to be pitied. And [my mother] was not out there preaching this, but in our house—everything that came into our house by way of the newspaper or the radio or talk about political candidates and so on was all *subversive*. Our house was subversive.

In another interview you talked about—and I guess I saw it in Down in My Heart *too—trying to get into a position where you were not angry, but at the same time able to be separate.*

Angry thoughts are not bright thoughts. Anger is not conducive to perception. That's part of the attitude. And, actually . . . one of the attitudes [of the pacifist] is: assume goodwill, but of course you're ready for non-goodwill. But you ought to start all over again, as often as you can, as long as you can, assuming goodwill again because it's not your purpose to overwhelm or overcome—well, overcome in that song, but overcome by understanding, by kindness, by show- ing them that it's in their interest to act right. They don't know that and it's very easy to fly off the handle because they don't, but it doesn't help them and it doesn't help you, really.

It's a position of power. It's moral jujitsu, and the more aggressive they are, the more vulnerable they are. [But] it's not right, I think, to tease authorities into doing dumb things. I had that problem during the Vietnam War because one of the tactics was to get the authorities to overreact. I don't want them to overreact; I want them to act right. So calling them "the Fuzz," daring them to do things; that's not our way. But on the other hand, it isn't our way to do things that we don't think to be right.

Didn't you ever have trouble with that? Did you ever get angry and then have to back down?

Oh, yes, yes, you get angry; yes, yes, we're animals. But it's not my best self. What I'm voicing is not so much an achieved position as a desired position. My mother had that, but she had it naturally. I have it sort of intellectually, if I can use that without being vaunting about it. I mean it's a *perception* on my part. . . .

. . . You didn't want to be as trusting as your father. . . . You were glad that you had some of your mother's fear.

Yes, my father was too heroic. I don't mean a great hero, I just mean that he had those attitudes that say if you're tough enough, you can make it enough, and I don't believe that. That is not the intellectual perception I have of the conditions of life. And it hurts me when I hear writers, the tough people, prevailing over an audience by voicing what seem to me to be specious arguments, sort of the heroic stance: "Lean on the Nicaraguans hard enough and they'll be nice like us" — I don't believe that for a minute. . . .

. . . As a kid I was impressed by what [my father] could hear, what he could see, and what he was ready to listen for. So listening is a kind of epitome of what I felt about my father, about that readiness to learn from what's coming in from outside. He's hearing it, he's sifting it in, and he's getting whatever signals there are, which is a very strong position, I think. . . .

It's only lately that I've come to realize from talking to other people—of course everyone's family is different—that the distinction of our family was this mutual reinforcement of an attitude toward danger or toward aggression or even toward evil which was that of redemption. . . . You don't overwhelm the opposition, you don't wipe them out; you redeem them, you save them. They can count on you. You don't always count on them, but you always try to get into the attitude that you're ready to count on them; but you're also ready, if necessary, to oppose them, but oppose them the way Martin Luther King did, the way Gandhi did. Those are our heroes. Actually, I guess this is a religious position. It's a Quaker, Mennonite, Brethren, Buddha position. And in a way, in the fast terminology to use, a kind of feminine position.

From "People Are Equal," an interview by Nancy Bunge, published in Kansas Quarterly 24, no. 4 and vol. 25, no. 1 (1993).

———

ALL THEIR TIME THINKING

A Letter to the Editor

Strangely, I was once a part of a group confronted by police late at night in L.A. We were COs in World War II waiting for a ride back to camp. We were taunted and goaded in an effort to get us to do something actionable. But we didn't oblige. Maybe we helped defuse some of the anger built up in the job of policing? Somehow we must get out of that reciprocal "solution."

—from Stafford's letter to Jordan Jones, the editor of
Bakunin, *submitted with the following interview and published as "An Interview with William Stafford."*

INTERVIEWER: *Do you think there are any . . . problems being a professor-poet?*

STAFFORD: Many problems, many problems. I go back to universities and colleges now, I walk down the hall, and I hear the professors lecturing as I did for years, and I get kind of a smothered feeling. I get this feeling, "Oh really? Do people really know that much?" There's something about the positions of it or the tone of this talking down to people that becomes natural to being a professor. I speak as a sinner, you know. I was a professor, and I knew everything. Well, I've gradually come to realize that, no, I really didn't know everything. I just talked as if I knew everything. There are all those aspects, areas, emphases that none of us understands. I've become more aware of that.

. . . "Traveling through the Dark," I think one of your more anthologized poems, has that gesture at the end where you "thought hard for us all."

Yeah, you do know that poem. Well that gesture of conciliation is a pretty handy thing to come in here. I feel when I'm writing that in anyone's life there must be certain currents that are of overwhelming importance. And in my own life and experience, I realize now after all these years that very important to me is that same feeling I voiced just a minute ago about walking down the hall and hearing people from on high lecturing other people. That's not the way it is. People are equal. In any room there isn't one person who has it. There is a room full of people who all have it from their point of view. And so, there aren't enemies. We all see a certain side of experience. And I keep trying to find that and reach out: conciliation, that gesture. I've been a member of the Fellowship of Reconciliation for fifty years . . . and that permeates my life. I guess it gets into my writing. . . .

. . . Your time as a conscientious objector during World War II . . . Did you immediately apply to be a conscientious objector?

Yes, but I had a draft board that sure didn't want me to go higher, to appeal my draft status. They didn't want to spoil their record by having a CO. At the draft hearing someone had a little poem to read to me, some demeaning thing. And there were even a lot of threats to me. And so I just listened. I took it. And they said, "Is there anyone who can swear to you having this position before the war?" I thought about it and I said, "Well, yes, come to think of it, the commander of the American Legion in El Dorado, Kansas, can because I've argued with him for years." So they got in touch with him, and he was my best witness.

So it was easy for you?

Yes it was, but some of them had a really hard time. Some were stampeded into the military. Sylvan Waibright was denied his status. He was from a Brethren community, but one of the draft boards said, "Sylvan, you can't be a CO, I know that you go to dances." That means he's not a good Brethren somehow. Sylvan said, "Yeah, I'll dance, but I won't kill." . . .

Then there were a couple who had unusual answers for their draft boards. There was a fellow named Hidarro Herrera from Coyote, New Mexico, and he could speak a little English, and I asked him about his draft board. He said they asked him, "Why are you refusing to go to war?" And he said, "God don't like war." So, where do you go from there? What could you ask next? And then Klamath Jackson was an Indian in our camp, and when they called him up, he said, "My tribe's not at war." So they sent him to a CO camp.

Was it hard to prove that you were really a conscientious objector, that you really didn't believe in war?

Even the way you put this gives me an opening to say something that I learned when I was a CO, and that is, you don't have to go. Most people say that if you don't go they'll put you in prison. The CO says, so what? OK, I'm ready. A CO is a person who refuses to go to war. That's it.

So if you were able to get CO status, then what happened to you?

The government established Civilian Public Service camps for the COs, alternative service for those who "by reason of their religious training or belief were conscientiously opposed to war." I was not a member of any church, which gave my draft board a few fits. All sorts of people finally filtered into the camps. I mean, the government didn't want to try to define religion. They didn't want to get into that, and they didn't want to tangle with people who were just going to be obstreperous in the army. So, generally, relations with the rational part of the military proved to be fairly serene. Enlightened people want things to go well.

Were there different types of service COs could go into?

Oh yes. Some worked in mental hospitals, some were guinea pigs in starvation experiments at the University of Minnesota, some were in hot and cold rooms, in experiments on how people survive under extreme conditions. Later in my service, I was assigned to helping the education division of the Brethren, and I traveled to various places. I visited someone in the hot room at the University of Michigan, and he had just gotten out of the cold room the week before.

That reminds me of the Nazi doctors' testing of Jews and Gypsies.

But you didn't have to do that. You could volunteer. Those in the starvation experiment were starved way down, like guys who were 150 pounds would be 100 pounds. I mean right down to skeletons. Morris Keaton visited the starvation experiment with me and he said, "Those guys are just about gone." And they found out that when men are starving, they're unreliable no matter what their principles were. They had volunteered to help mankind, but they couldn't be let out by the scientist while they were on the starvation experiment because they'd get into the garbage cans and eat. I mean, it just gets you.

A pretty hard gig to be a CO. What kind of service did you do?

I was first sent to an alternative service camp run by the Church of the Brethren at Magnolia, Arkansas. And there were a hundred and some COs there. We converged from various places, all the way from the hills, Harvard, wherever. The guy next to me in the barracks had just gotten his Ph.D. in philosophy from Harvard, and the guy down the row was from the hills of Kentucky. Listening to those two talk was fascinating. The first night, the fellow from Kentucky came up and said to Morris Keaton, who was the Ph.D., "Well, where do you work?" And Keaton said, "I just graduated from Harvard." And this fellow from Kentucky said, "Oh, you ain't never worked, have you?" Sort of brought things down to the right level at the beginning.

What was the mood of the country toward the war and toward COs?

Our society was more divided over the issue of the war than most people remember. And then Pearl Harbor stampeded almost everybody, and I remember listening to Roosevelt do his "Day of Infamy" speech the day after. But even after that there was still quite a number of people who weren't in it. . . .

So people felt it was patriotic to act out in violence against anyone who disagreed with the government? That seems a little ironic in a war to save democracy.

I'll tell you, later on, when I was in a camp in California, a couple of Forest Service men were talking to the COs one night about being patriotic. One of them said, "Well you guys, you're not doing anything for the war effort. I want you to know that right after the war was declared, I went with some other fellows and we killed a German spy right here." One of the COs said, "Killed? How did you know he was a spy?" "Well, we had word, and we killed him, and I'm just telling you. Others don't know about this, but we did it, I mean, we're for real." One of the guys said, "You can't do that. It's unconstitutional." And this Forest Service man said, "Young man, when it's a matter of patriotism, I don't care whether it's constitutional or not." . . .

As I understand it, you were able to have classes in the camps. Is that true?

There was a little building and we had all our books together, and we called that our library. We did the best we could. We had classes going in which anyone who knew a lot would teach a class. For example, Morris Keaton taught philosophy. He later taught philosophy at Antioch. The work was hard. We'd go out at dawn and—I started to say line up, though that really didn't work. The first project director said, "Fall in!" and the COs just looked at each other wondering, "Who is this guy? What does he think this is?" So we sort of shuffled our feet, and he looked down at his paper again, and he decided not to push it. Anyway, we'd go out early, work hard, and come home and try to have our classes, but we'd be tired. So we had this bright idea—which I still practice as a writer—which was we'd get up at four A.M. and do our classes and our reading while we were fresh, and then when we were exhausted we'd work for the government.

. . . The poets of [the San Francisco Renaissance after the war] were known not just for their pacifism and leftism but for the whole concept of the politically engaged artist, which was frowned upon by the detached, impersonal university poets of the period. Were most COs well educated?

They had education statistics, and the COs were way up there because a lot of them were intellectuals. Mostly that's the kind of people who had the imagination to think the world might end with an unbelievable bomb, which turned out to be true. So I was thinking about that this morning, that going to war shows a lack of imagination. I mean by the end of the war we had done things that I don't think most people in my generation would have said any American would ever do—the bombing of Dresden, the bomb at Hiroshima. Now we have come to accept these things—defoliation of Vietnam, mass destruction. But the COs could and did imagine it. They had the imagination. They spent all their time thinking and talking about it. One CO said to me, "A fellow came up to me and said I want to know your reason for being a CO," and this CO said, "You got a couple of hours to stand here and talk about this?" And when the fellow said no, the CO said, "Well, it will take that long." So they did a lot of talk, and their heroes were Gandhi and Tolstoy and so on, and many of them went into the Civil Rights movement right after the war. And it's important to remember, there were COs everywhere. Aldous Huxley, Bertrand Russell—he was in prison in World War I, he was a CO. The percentage of COs in England was greater than here in the United States, and it's strange because they were getting bombed. There were COs in Germany, everywhere.

From "An Interview with William Stafford," by Mitchell Smith, conducted in Santa Barbara on May 1 and 2, 1993, for The Writer's Gallery, *KCSB, University of California-Santa Barbara, and published in* Bakunin *5, no. 1 (Summer 1994).*

Notes to Some Poems

p. 3. "These Mornings." William Stafford wrote this poem at Los Prietos, a camp for conscientious objectors near Santa Barbara, California, during World War II.

p. 83. "Learning." William Stafford was born in 1914, and in his Kansas childhood he experienced both the patriotic fervor of World War I and public demonstrations by the Ku Klux Klan.

p. 84. "Explaining the Big One." Hitler, Stalin, Roosevelt, Churchill, and Eisenhower were players in a war drama that pacifists watched from the sidelines. As Stafford said in a poem written while he was in college, "It was hard to tell our protectors from the wolves."

p. 84. "At the Bomb Testing Site." An early draft of this poem appears as a frontispiece to this book, in which Stafford shows his welcome of ordinary language, and then his readiness to listen deeper to first utterance. In revision, for example, "something more than just waiting" becomes "The hands gripped hard on the desert." After revising, he submitted the poem to eleven magazines over four years before it was accepted. Like the lizard in his poem, his act of witness includes intuition, transformation, and absolute persistence.

p. 85. "At the Grave of My Brother: Bomber Pilot." William Stafford's younger brother, Bob, enlisted in the air force during World War II. Bob once said to his pacifist brother, Bill, "We're both heroes, Bill, but yours is a harder kind of hero."

p. 86. "A Message from the Wanderer." One of William Stafford's first published poems was titled "Communication from a Wanderer," written in the opening days of World War II. He spent the rest of his life writing, teaching, and traveling to witness for truth, peace, and reconciliation.

p. 87. "At the Un-National Monument along the Canadian Border." When Charles Kuralt was on a canoe trip in the boundary waters of northern Minnesota, his guide stopped the canoe at one point, took this poem out of his wallet, and read it aloud. "I always read this one when I get to the border," he said.

p. 88. "Peace Walk." Stafford took part in a sit-in on behalf of black students at the University of Kansas in the late 1930s, and later took part in peace demonstrations wherever he lived.

p. 89. "Watching the Jet Planes Dive." William Stafford kept going back to find the source of peace. He once wrote in his daily writing, "I am like a Greek chorus, speaking deliberately and measuredly the central truth of things, while all around me people—bankers, generals, kings, my children, everyone—all speak the wildest kind of impulsive, mistaken things."

p. 89. "A Ritual to Read to Each Other." This poem has been featured in national discussions of issues ranging from international diplomacy to the violence in our schools. Stafford saw the importance of clear signals in personal relationships and between nations. The mistranslation of a message from the Japanese government has been blamed for the decision to drop atomic bombs on Hiroshima and Nakasaki. Peace can depend on choosing exactly the right words.

p. 90. "Thinking for Berky." Stafford remembered many of the hard lives of friends from childhood. He had a special affinity for the "girl in the front row who had no mother" (from his poem "At Liberty School") or the "slow girl in art class, / less able to say where our lessons led . . ." (from "A Gesture Toward an Unfound Renaissance"). This habit may account for his own sense of isolation as a teacher and witness: "Right has a long and intricate name. / And the saying of it is a lonely thing" (from "Lit Instructor"). His sensitivity enabled him to see that "justice will take us millions of intricate moves"—that is, the sustained attention to clear and courageous daily action.

p. 91. "A Dedication." As a pacifist, William Stafford was surrounded by military endeavors. But those endeavors, at the same time, were surrounded by something older and more mysterious—the dedication of the makers of peace.

p. 92. "Men." Stafford told his children, "A philanthropist is someone who gives money away that he should be giving back." He could be resentful, even cynical, about the swaggering ways of the rich and powerful around him. His pacifism was compounded of fellow-feeling for children, women, the vanquished, and the dispossessed.

p. 93. "Entering History." For over fifty years, Stafford was a member of the Fellowship of Reconciliation, an international community of people working to create conditions for peace. "If you want peace, work for justice."

p. 94. "Objector." Stafford was classified as a conscientious objector in 1942 and spent the war years in internment camps, an experience he chronicled in his master's thesis at the University of Kansas. This became his first book, recently reprinted as *Down in My Heart: Peace Witness in Wartime* (Oregon State University Press, 1998).

p. 95. "Serving with Gideon." Because Stafford left his native Kansas after World War II, that place became for him a parable for the American drama between influence and honesty. As in many of his poems, there is a direct relation between individual domestic actions and social, even cosmic, outcomes: a cup, a handkerchief—right and wrong in the U.S.A.

p. 96. "For the Unknown Enemy." Stafford's poems could be like philosophic sculptures, monuments to new ways of thinking. While traveling, he would tell his children, "Don't forget to talk to strangers." How else could one get help or direction in the world?

p. 96. "Ground Zero [December 1982]." On several occasions, Stafford took part in "The Shadow Project" on Hiroshima Day, August 6, lying down on the pavement to portray a victim of the atomic attack of 1945. The outlines of the demonstrators were then marked in chalk on the pavement as a reminder of the disappeared.

p. 97. "Five A.M." Stafford's habit of running in the early morning hours became stubborn in his later years, as it took him longer and longer to achieve the distance he had set for himself when he was in his early sixties. This meant he had to get up even earlier in order to run and to write before dawn.

p. 98. "Poetry." On the eve of a trip while serving as Poetry Consultant to the Library of Congress in 1970, Stafford asked his colleagues if it would be possible to walk to National Airport. The answer was no: too many freeways, and then the Pentagon. Stafford walked anyway.

p. 98. "Something to Declare." A veteran of many border crossings, Stafford traveled light. For a journey lasting several days or for months, he took only a shoulder bag with a few clothes, his slim box of paper for daily writing, and his camera. His destinations were various: Poland, Egypt, Pakistan, India, Nepal, Iran . . .

p. 99. "Allegiances." All his life Stafford had a kind of patriotism for local life. From his Kansas boyhood to his life as writer, teacher, and traveler, his possessions were few and his allegiances to places, people, and ideas were deep.

p. 100. "Our Kind." When asked by interviewers what writer had most influenced him, Stafford's invariable reply was, "My mother's voice influenced me more than any writer." A retiring person in some ways, his mother had clear opinions about what was important and what was not. Stafford inherited this ability to be led by his own mind, and not by bold claims from "our leaders."

p. 101. "How It Is." When Stafford was drafted in 1942, he left his home town of Hutchinson, Kansas, for good. When he returned to visit after the war, as a pacifist he was not fully welcomed except by his family. One of his friends told him, "You ought to just be machine-gunned."

p. 101. "1940." Stafford's poetry collection that won the National Book Award was called *Traveling through the Dark*, and in many ways he saw his life as a passage through a kind of social darkness that began with World War I and World War II.

p. 102. "In Camp." Years after World War II, when a fellow CO—a "saint from the kingdom," as they called each other—would visit, Stafford reported to his children that he felt a kind of light fill the room. "I don't know if others feel this," he said, "but I do."

p. 102. "Ground Zero [June 1982]." In his poem "Why I Am Happy," Stafford reports ". . . a lake somewhere / so blue and far nobody owns it." As a creator, he had access to something independent of history and hopelessness: "That lake stays blue and free; it goes / on and on. / And I know where it is."

p. 103. "The Animal That Drank Up Sound." When Stafford shared this poem with a writer in Tehran during the reign of the Shah, his friend expressed amazement that such an outright challenge to censorship could be permitted by any government, even in America. "Your poems are so political," the friend told him.

Is this poem, in fact, a political document? It may be the most autobiographical account Stafford ever wrote of the pacifist's quiet, essential, utterly direct and simple work of witness in a dangerous world. The poem was later published as a children's book, with illustrations by Debra Frasier.

p. 105. "The Star in the Hills." Stafford was a lifelong witness for the complex task of full citizenship in the world—the natural world, the world of many cultures, the world of the imagination. Would he take the loyalty oath when he taught in California? Well, yes, and then he would write a poem about what that oath meant.

p. 106. "Clash." Stafford wrote this mysterious poem in the 1950s. There is no evidence the drama described has anything to do with his actual family, but instead the action evokes the central drama of his life, his encounter with "mother country." He did not need to kill anyone, once he learned his freedom.

p. 108. "November." Stafford often took part in memorial gatherings on Hiroshima Day for readings and discussions of war and peace. In the last month of his life, he wrote this poem instead of attending the public events in Portland.

p. 108. "'Are You Mr. William Stafford?'" On the last day
of his life, Stafford wrote a poem that seems to sum up his
sense of the predicament of a human being. He is denied
certainty, but blessed with a sense of engagement with whatever comes. He departed in the flow of creation. His last act
as a writer may have been to put brackets around the word
"still": "I'm [still] here writing it down."

p. 109. "Family Statement." A poem written while Stafford
was in a CO camp during World War II. Stafford and his
brother, Bob, the bomber pilot, remained great friends
throughout the war, faithfully writing to one another about
the odd events of war from both sides of the soldier/pacifist
divide.

p. 110. "December." In many of his poems, the Stafford nar-
rator is alone. "I thought hard for us all . . . ," he says in his
poem "Traveling through the Dark." He was a wanderer,
partly because of the exile World War II imposed on a free-
thinker from Kansas, and partly because he was an active
witness for writing and reconciliation.

p. 115. "For the Oregon House Session, 13 April 1987."
When Governor Tom McCall named William Stafford the
Poet Laureate of Oregon in 1975, the deal between them
was "no pay, no duties." But there was one annual custom:
Stafford was to open each session of the legislature with a
poem. A prayer was not allowed, but a poem would serve.

William E. Stafford
1914–1993

William Stafford was born in Hutchinson, Kansas, in 1914.
In his early years he worked as a laborer in the sugar beet
fields, in construction, and at an oil refinery. He completed his bachelor's degree in English from the University
of Kansas in 1937. A conscientious objector and pacifist, he
spent 1942 through 1946 in Civilian Public Service camps
and at social agencies in Arkansas, California, Indiana, and
Illinois, fighting forest fires, building and maintaining trails
and roads, and training for postwar relief work. After the war
he taught high school, worked as secretary to the director of
Church World Service, and completed his master's degree
at the University of Kansas, submitting as his thesis his first
book, *Down in My Heart,* an account of war experience as a
conscientious objector. In 1948 he joined the English faculty
of Lewis & Clark College in Portland, where he taught inter-
mittently until his retirement in 1978.

Married to Dorothy Hope Frantz in 1944 and the father
of four children, Stafford authored sixty-seven volumes of
poetry and prose. His first poetry collection, *West of Your
City,* was published when he was forty-six. In addition to
the 1963 National Book Award for *Traveling through the*

Dark, Stafford's many honors included the Shelley Memorial Award from the Poetry Society of America and his appointment from 1970 to 1971 as Consultant in Poetry for the Library of Congress. In 1975 he was appointed Oregon Poet Laureate by Governor Tom McCall. Widely known for his habit of writing daily in the early morning, Stafford was an enormously loved and admired writer and a generous mentor to aspiring poets everywhere. He traveled thousands of miles to give workshops and readings throughout the United States and abroad, in Egypt, India, Bangladesh, Nepal, Pakistan, Iran, Germany, Austria, Japan, and Poland. He died at his home in Lake Oswego, Oregon, in August of 1993.

Other Sources for Information about William Stafford and Pacifism

Books

Andrews, Tom, ed. *On William Stafford: The Worth of Local Things.* Ann Arbor: University of Michigan Press, 1993.

Holden, Jonathan. *The Mark to Turn: A Reading of William Stafford's Poetry.* Lawrence: University Press of Kansas, 1976.

Kitchen, Judith. *Writing the World: Understanding William Stafford.* Corvallis: Oregon State University Press, 1999.

Stafford, Kim. *Early Morning: Remembering My Father, William Stafford.* St. Paul, Minn.: Graywolf Press, 2002.

Stafford, William. *The Answers Are Inside the Mountains.* Ann Arbor: University of Michigan Press, 2003.

———. *Crossing Unmarked Snow: Further Views on the Writer's Vocation.* Ann Arbor: University of Michigan Press, 1998.

———. *Down in My Heart: Peace Witness in Wartime.* With an introduction by Kim Stafford. Corvallis: Oregon State University Press, 1998.

———. *The Way It Is: New and Selected Poems.* St. Paul, Minn.: Graywolf Press, 1998.

———. *Even in Quiet Places.* Afterword by Kim Stafford. Lewiston, Idaho: Confluence Press, 1994.

Videos

The Good War and Those Who Refused to Fight It. Produced
and directed by Rick Tejada-Flores and Judith Ehrlich.
Paradigm Productions, 2000. A video documentary about
the COs in World War II.

William Stafford and Robert Bly: A Literary Friendship.
Produced and directed by Haydn Reiss. Reiss Films, 1994.
A video documentary.

William Stafford: What the River Says. Produced and directed by Michael Markee and Vincent Wixon. TTTD
Productions, 1989.

Organizations

The Estate of William Stafford, P.O. Box 80595, Portland,
Oreg. 97280-1595, www.lclark.edu/~krs/archive.html.

Fellowship of Reconciliation, P.O. Box 271, Nyack, N.Y.
10960.

Friends of William Stafford, P.O. Box 592, Lake Oswego,
Oreg. 97034, www.williamstafford.org.

Acknowledgments

This book could not have been compiled without generous help. First, I would like to thank Emilie Buchwald at Milkweed Editions for her welcoming response when I first asked about what we might do in the face of the events of September 11, 2001. The support of Milkweed for this project was clear and sustained as we created a book with both literary and cultural purposes.

Second, I would like to thank Fiona McCrae and the staff at Graywolf Press for allowing us to reprint poems from Graywolf's *The Way It Is: New and Selected Poems* by William Stafford. These include "A Dedication," "A Message from the Wanderer," "A Ritual to Read to Each Other," "Allegiances," "'Are You Mr. William Stafford?'" "At the Bomb Testing Site," "At the Grave of My Brother: Bomber Pilot," "At the Un-National Monument along the Canadian Border," "Clash," "Entering History," "Explaining the Big One," "Five A.M.," "For the Unknown Enemy," "Ground Zero [June 1982]," "Ground Zero [December 1982]," "How It Is," "In Camp," "Learning," "1940," "November," "Objector," "Our Kind," "Peace Walk," "Serving with Gideon," "Something to Declare," "The Animal That Drank Up Sound," "The Star in the Hills," "Thinking for Berky," and "Watching the Jet Planes Dive." Without these poems, this book would lack an important dimension. Thanks to both Confluence Press, for allowing us to reprint "Atwater Kent" from *How to Hold Your Arms When It Rains* and "Men," "Poetry," and "Pretend You Live in a Room" from *Even in Quiet Places,* and to the University of Michigan Press, for the use of "For the Oregon House Session" from *Crossing Unmarked Snow* and "You and Art" from *You Must Revise Your Life.* Thanks also to the editors of magazines and small presses where some of the other poems and texts in this book were first published.

Third, I would like to thank Paul Merchant and Diane McDevitt at the William Stafford Archive, and particularly Vince and Patty Wixon and the other volunteers there for typing texts from my father's daunting handwriting and helping to select appropriate poetry and prose for this book. Paul and Vince have been persistent in their preparation of this and other books imaginatively drawn from the Archive.

Finally, I thank my family for their support in this work. Many days I have spent more time with my father, ten years gone, than with my dear ones close by. This is another way to be together: that our children may inherit a world rich in the spirit of reconciliation.

Born in Portland, Oregon, in 1949, KIM STAFFORD grew up following his parents as they moved from Oregon to Iowa, Indiana, California, Alaska, and back to Oregon. He attended the University of Oregon for twelve years, eventually earning a Ph.D. in medieval literature. His publications include *Having Everything Right: Essays of Place,* which won a Western States Book Award in 1986. His most recent books are *Early Morning: Remembering My Father, William Stafford* and *The Muses Among Us: Eloquent Listening and Other Pleasures of the Writer's Craft.*

He serves as literary executor for the Estate of William Stafford, and directs the Northwest Writing Institute at Lewis & Clark College, where he has taught since 1979. He lives in Portland with his wife and children.

Brown Dog of the Yaak:
Essays on Art and Activism
Rick Bass

Changing the Bully Who Rules the World:
Reading and Thinking about Ethics
Carol Bly

Outsiders:
Poems about Rebels, Exiles, and Renegades
Edited by Laure-Anne Bosselaar

The Tree of Red Stars
Tessa Bridal

Transforming a Rape Culture
Edited by Emilie Buchwald, Pamela Fletcher, and Martha Roth

The Colors of Nature:
Culture, Identity, and the Natural World
Edited by Alison H. Deming and Lauret E. Savoy

The Children Bob Moses Led
William Heath

The Old Bridge:
The Third Balkan War and the Age of the Refugee
Christopher Merrill

An American Child Supreme:
The Education of a Liberation Ecologist
John Nichols

The Barn at the End of the World:
The Apprenticeship of a Quaker, Buddhist Shepherd
Mary Rose O'Reilley

Wild Card Quilt:
Taking a Chance on Home
Janisse Ray

Cracking India
Bapsi Sidhwa

White Flash/Black Rain:
Women of Japan Relive the Bomb
Edited by Lequita Vance-Watkins and Aratani Mariko

MILKWEED EDITIONS publishes with the intention of making a humane impact on society, in the belief that literature is a transformative art uniquely able to convey the essential experiences of the human heart and spirit. To that end, Milkweed publishes distinctive voices of literary merit in handsomely designed, visually dynamic books, exploring the ethical, cultural, and esthetic issues that free societies need continually to address. Milkweed Editions is a not-for-profit press.

JOIN US

Since its genesis as *Milkweed Chronicle* in 1979, Milkweed has helped hundreds of emerging writers reach their readers. Thanks to the generosity of foundations and of individuals like you, Milkweed Editions is able to continue its nonprofit mission of publishing books chosen on the basis of literary merit—the effect they have on the human heart and spirit—rather than on the basis of how they impact the bottom line. That's a miracle that our readers have made possible.

In addition to purchasing Milkweed books, you can join the growing community of Milkweed supporters. Individual contributions of any amount are both meaningful and welcome. Contact us for a Milkweed catalog or log on to www.milkweed.org and click on "About Milkweed," then "Supporting Milkweed," to find out about our donor program, or simply call (800) 520-6455 and ask about becoming one of Milkweed's contributors. As a nonprofit press, Milkweed belongs to you, the community. Milkweed's board, its staff, and especially the authors whose careers you help launch thank you for reading our books and supporting our mission in any way you can.

Interior design by Christian Fünfhausen.
Typeset in 11/15 point Garamond
by Stanton Publication Services.